«Dr. Tamburri has done what we all need to do: learn how the past has created the present so that we can better face the challenges the future brings. Through this study, he helps us better know our place in this world of identity politics, so that when we think, we can act on knowledge more than sentiment, and when we act, we can create opportunities to make this world a better place for everyone. Through thorough research, logical argumentation, and careful articulation, Tamburri creates a document that wisely speaks to the needs of all Americans and provides a blueprint of how we can build new ways toward peaceful coexistence of all, no matter your political persuasion. This is must reading for all Italian Americans».

Dr. Fred L. Gardaphé
Distinguished Professor of English & Italian American Studies
Queens College, The City University of New York

«Once again, Professor Tamburri takes on an area of ethnic self–reflection that most avoid. Calling the politics of [self–]omission a challenge to the Italian/American community is an understatement. This much needed volume serves as a reiteration that understanding a culture's ethnic past is critical to having a national political voice in the present, especially given the increasing weight given to the politics of identity. To understand and preserve an authentic Italian/American cultural identity, the narrative cannot be rewritten toward personal interest and those exhorting a particular brand of ethnic identity based on self–interest must know their history and use this to support their arguments rather than emotions aroused by a misguided sense of ethnic pride. Instead of ignoring deleterious aspects of the past, Italian Americans are obligated to learn about these and work toward resolving such issues in a way that neither diminishes nor demeans other racial and ethnic groups. Tamburri reminds us that Giovanni Schiavo was addressing such questions in the first half of the 20th century and that the ways to change the situation lie in education by developing courses and curricula in Italian/American and Italian Diaspora Studies. Although little progress has been made in that regard, the present discussion is a call to action for the Italian/American community to finally do what is required to ensure the work is finally accomplished».

Donna Chirico, Professor of Psychology
York College, The City University of New York

Welfare comunitario

Politiche locali, sviluppo e mutamento sociale

6

Welfare comunitario

Politiche locali, sviluppo e mutamento sociale

Welfare comunitario vuole essere un "luogo" di confronto sul tema del rapporto tra la società, con le sue diverse sfaccettature, e l'attore sociale, con le sue realizzazioni plastiche e anche con quelle non tangibili. La collana si offre come momento di autoascolto sul mutamento sociale *tout–court* e propone spunti di riflessione attraverso la connessione tra la ricerca sociologica e le sue ricadute empiriche, mediante attività di ricerca applicata. Le proposte di pubblicazione saranno sottoposte a un sistema *(blind)* di *peer review*.

ANTHONY JULIAN **TAMBURRI**

A POLITICS
OF [SELF–]OMISSION
THE ITALIAN/AMERICAN CHALLENGE
IN A POST–GEORGE FLOYD AGE

aracne

aracne

©

ISBN
979–12–218–0284–9

USA Edition
ISBN 978-1-955995-04-7

Connecticut • May 2025

Casa Lago Press
www.casalagopress.org

FIRST EDITION
ROMA 27 OCTOBER 2022

O natura, o natura,
Perché non rendi poi
Quel che prometti allor? perché di tanto
Inganni i figli tuoi?

A Silvia, G. LEOPARDI
19–20 April 1828

TABLE OF CONTENTS

PART III

ACKNOWLEDGEMENTS

Some of the chapters herein have been previously published and appear now either in their original form or modified for this venue. The following four essays have appeared before:

- *The Semiotics of Labeling: "Italian" to "American", "Non–white" to "White", and Other Privileges of Choosing* first appeared in *Circolazione di persone e di idee: Integrazione ed esclusione tra Europa e Americhe*. Sabrina Vellucci and Susanna Nanni, eds. Bordighera Press, 2019. It appears here slightly expanded.
- *The Columbus Controversy and the Politics of Omission* first appeared in «La Voce di New York», December, 17, 2017.
- *Indro Montanelli: Reverence Misdirected?* also first appeared in «La Voce di New York», June, 24, 2020.
- *Why Promotors of Italian/American Culture Need to Know More: The Italian/American Experience in Religion*

first appeared in the «Journal of Religion and Society», 24, 2022. It appears here notably expanded.

I thank first and foremost the directors of Bordighera Press and «La Voce di New York» to be able to reprint the four chapters here in modified form. I also wish to thank Stephen Cerulli, Donna Chirico, Fred L. Gardaphé, Joseph Sciorra, Michele d'Egidio Tamburri, and Sabrina Vellucci. They have all contributed in various and sundry ways to the thinking as well as the formation of ideas herein expressed. Maria, of course, always allows the time.

Of course, any fallacies, perceived or real, are mine.

INTRODUCTION
WHY NOW

The idea for this book was born out of discussions that originated after the murder of George Floyd. Until then, the 2017 brouhaha in New York City surrounding the Christopher Columbus statue seemed to have faded a bit from collective memory. At that time, in 2017, then Speaker of New York City's City Council Melissa Mark–Viverito had called for the reconsideration of the Columbus statue's value, and if it should not be included among the so–called "hate statues". Yes, people subsequently continued to discuss Columbus, but not to the degree and with the heated passion we have since witnessed post–George Floyd's murder.

While some of the chapters herein pre–date the Floyd murder and the subsequent discussions and protests, I believe that they nonetheless prove relevant in any discussion on the "Columbus Affair", as I have called it, and all that it pertains[1]. How we see ourselves (chapter 1), how we

---

(1) For more on Columbus, see Tamburri (2021).

might characterize the behavior of others (chapter 2 and 3), and how we have constructed mis–guided, alternative narratives (chapters 4 and 5) constitute a rainbow of issues that call for remedies in order for Italian Americans to move forward in a more constructive manner, are all part and parcel to any discussion — Columbus or more general — on Italians in America. Nothing should be left on the cutting–room floor.

In his ground–breaking essay, *Breaking the Silence: Strategic Imperatives for Italian American Culture*, Robert Viscusi championed an articulation of history that includes a collective purpose. While much progress has been made on numerous issues, many Italian/American associations seem to continue to work in a vacuum, moving forward alone on issues; whereas were more groups to work in unison, the Italian/American population at large would benefit, thus encountering greater success in bringing forth a variety of projects that would contribute to an Italian/American agenda.

What is — or what should be — that rallying point around which Italian Americans might find some sense of commonality? Indeed, both African Americans and Jewish Americans have, respectively, their one issue, as tragic as it may be, that coheres the group. I have in mind, of course, slavery and its dreadful sister of outright discrimination that has resulted from it, for the former; two millennia of *diasporic* existence and the horrific twentieth–century holocaust, for the latter.

What then can we identify as that cohesive force for Italian Americans? Can we look to something like immigration, that timespan from 1880 to 1924, those forty–four years that have now become an historical marker for contemporary Italian Americans? There may indeed also be specific tragedies that come to mind: the 1891 New Orleans lynching, for which we hold the dubious distinction of having been victims of the largest single "white" lynching[2]. One might even underscore historical discrimination, dating back to the nineteenth century and culminating, to date, in something like *Everyone Loves Raymond* or *The Sopranos*.

Though valid points of discussion, these last two examples do not constitute, in an encompassing manner, that one issue that can unite the Italian/American population in the same way in which other groups cohere. We might thus ponder what is that all encompassing issue that unites, for instance, Latinx. In addition to a strong sense of belonging they may have with regard to their culture(s), it may very well be the migratory experience — a sense of not belonging to the host country — that coheres Latinx. Surely, I do not want to be naïve in thinking that Latinx from any and all Latin/American countries have an equal sense of allegiance to the "old country". Nor do I want to imply that all Latinx have an automatic sense of belonging to that group comprised of Latinx, as categorized in the United States. Nevertheless, we would not err in perceiving a certain sense of commonality that has its origins in the migratory experience insofar as they perceive themselves as outsiders, and, as such, hold on to their culture of origins. This combination of difference and cultural specificity — based in part on the migratory experience — surely figures as a cohering agent.

---

(2) After one hundred twenty–eight years, the City of New Orleans issued a formal apology. For details, see Ryan Prior. Indeed, we had to wait for an African/American female mayor for someone in office who could truly empathize with this historical tragedy. On the New Orleans lynching, see Daniela G. Jäger; on the general history of lynchings of Italians in the United States, see Patrizia Salvetti.

An analogous formula might prove thus valid for Italian Americans. Immigration and its more than century–long history may very well figure as part of that cohesive agent, however tenuous. A strong sense of commonality is a necessary ingredient for the population to cohere and thus to progress for the study of all things Italian/American to become part and parcel of the *mainstream*, as it is for other United States hyphenated groups. To be sure, one added challenge is that there is greater distance between us Italian Americans and our migratory history, and therefore we need to make that extra effort to bridge that knowledge gap and, in the end, also correct some of the narratives we often hear, one being the question of "legal" *vs.* "illegal" historical Italian immigration. Hence, in addition to such thinking in a one–way and chronologically based mind–set, we might, in the end, consider the more complex legacy of said history. In so doing, we enter the realm of diasporic studies, the consideration of the dispersal of Italians beyond Italy's border, in our case the United States, and how such a legacy has created new, contemporary articulations of the Italian–descendent populations throughout the United States as well as other parts of world[3].

All of this is dependent on an Italian/American commitment (*impegno*) to the appreciation of our culture. This entails an active participation in cultural activities of all sorts; it requires that Italian/American groups make a concerted effort to go beyond those one or two activities they have identified as their own and make attempts to expand their agenda to include a new, more encompassing form of

---

(3) The idea of speaking in terms of diaspora and not just immigration and its legacy was born out of a conversation with Stephen Cerulli, in which he insisted that we need to adhere to something not just historical but, indeed, current as well. See my essay (TAMBURRI 2022).

cultural integration. All of this is dependent on a combination of cultural awareness and appreciation: namely, a new sense of the Italian/American self that ultimately leads to an appropriation of and identification with one's cultural legacy.

A concerted *conversation* ("cum vetere": i.e., coming together) on cultural philanthropy among Italian Americans is, I would submit, something necessary to bring to the table. The concept has yet to be discussed beyond those few occasions among a small number of individuals. We need only turn to (1) names on libraries, colleges of arts and humanities, and privately endowed professorships, (2) the lack of a free–standing *national* museum, and (3) graduate programs in Italian Americana, for us to realize how far behind we are in cultural appreciation.

Works Cited

Jäger D.G., 2002, *The Worst 'White Lynching' in American History: Elites vs. Italians in New Orleans, 1891*, «AAA: Arbeiten aus Anglistik und Amerikanistik», 2.2: 161–179.

Prior R., 2019, *128 years later, New Orleans is apologizing for lynching 11 Italians*, «CNN», https://www.cnn.com/2019/04/01/us/new–orleans–mayor–apologizes–italian–americans–trnd/index.html.

Salvetti P., 2017, *Rope and Soap: Lynchings of Italians in the United States*, trans. Fabio Girelli Carasi, Bordighera Press, New York.

Tamburri A.J., 2022a, *Italian Diaspora Studies and the University: Professional development, Curricular Matters, Cultural Philanthropy*, Bordighera Press, New York.

TAMBURRI A.J., 2022b, *Italian Diasporic Studies: The Then and Now*, «Diasporic Italy», 2.

TAMBURRI A.J., 2021, *The Columbus Affair: Imperatives for an Italian/American Agenda*, CT: Casa Lago Press, New Fairfield.

VISCUSI R., 1990, *Breaking the Silence: Strategic Imperatives for Italian American Culture*, «Voices in Italian Americana», 1.1, (Spring): 1–13.

PART I

THE SEMIOTICS OF LABELING
"ITALIAN" TO "AMERICAN", "NON–WHITE"
TO "WHITE", AND OTHER PRIVILEGES OF CHOOSING

When we approach notions of "Italian", "American", and/or "whiteness", we find ourselves on a most slippery slope. This is not to discourage the study of such subject matter. On the contrary, immigrants of southern European origins have not always been considered white, and as a result, those of the great migration from Italy who hailed from below the "Linea Spezia" were in fact placed into a non–white category for a period of time. Let us remember that Italians were sometimes clustered with Blacks in excluding them from employment[1].

More intriguing in this history of the racialized Italian is the appeal of Rollins *vs.* State in Alabama. An African American, Jim Rollins had engaged in a relationship with an Italian/American woman. Given the anti–miscegenation laws of the time, Rollins was tried for and found guilty of race mixing: «The defendant was convicted of miscegenation under an indictment which charges that Edith Labue, a white person, and Jim Rollins alias, etc., a negro or descendant of a negro, did intermarry or live in adultery

---

(1) For more on whiteness and ethnics in the U.S., two works to consult are David Roediger and Matthew Jacobson.

or fornication with each other, etc.»[2]. Rollins appealed, and a year later the court decided in his favor. However, in granting his appeal, the Court stated:

> There was no competent evidence to show that the woman in question, Edith Labue, was a white woman, or that she did not have negro blood in her veins and was not the descendant of a negro. This fact was essential to a conviction in this case, and, like any other material ingredient of the offense must be proven by the evidence beyond a reasonable doubt and to a moral certainty. The mere fact that the testimony showed this woman came from Sicily can in no sense be taken as conclusive that she was therefore a white woman, or that she was not a negro or a descendant of a negro.[3]

A southern Italian, indeed, a Sicilian woman, emphatically underscores the dominant culture's perceived non–whiteness of Edith Labue, as determined by the 1922 Court of Appeals of Alabama; thus, "in no sense", we read above, could she be considered "a *white* woman", or would one conclude "that she was not a *negro* or a *descendant of a negro*" (my emphasis). The decisiveness of the decision is evident; and hence, according to such legal determination, the Italian of this era could not enjoy the privilege of whiteness. Indeed, such laws appeared in the statutes of most states until the U.S. Supreme Court struck them down in 1967 (Haney López, esp. 82–85)[4].

---

(2) Accessed 6 February 2019: https://casetext.com/case/rollins–v–state–120. I wish to thank Jessica Barbata Jackson for first bringing this to our attention in her book on Italians in a Jim Crow South (2020).

(3) Accessed 6 February 2019: https://casetext.com/case/rollins–v–state–120.

(4) During this same period, Robert F. Forester wrote: «Contempt, or at best contemptuous tolerance, prompts the vernacular epithets "Wop",

All this to say that our obligation to negotiate said slippery slope seems inevitable, it is a commitment for both the scholar and the community leader, as we re–interrogate the racial and social history of the Italian immigrants in our respective host countries[5]. Undoubtedly, if we understand more fully our own migratory history and its challenges, we could better understand the current phenomena associated with immigration today. In deciding to engage in such discussions one inevitably runs the risk of falling into a trap of flat, superficial analysis that ultimately eschews the complexities of both ethnicity and "whiteness", or any other term under examination. As a result, the multi–strata characteristic, for example, of any "white" ethnic group fades out and an incomplete portrait of the group results. In order to avoid this, we must let go of some of our traditional historical–thematic perspectives that reign still among certain dominant culturalists, or within what are now nicely bleached, "white" ethnic communities[6].

What I shall do in what follows is to explore some labels ascribed to Italian immigrants and their progeny and examine such terminology about any consequences such labels might signify.

"Guinea", and "Dago". In a country where yet the distinction between white man and black is intended as a distinction of value as well as in ethnography it is no compliment to the Italian to deny him his whiteness, but that actually happens with considerable frequency» (408).

(5) The United States is not alone in its history of racial strife and Italians. One example is Australia and its determination to remain a "white" country, especially during the years of turmoil of the early 1960s.

(6) Regarding whiteness and Italian Americans, see, first and foremost, Jennifer Guglielmo and Salvatore Salerno's *Are Italians White?* This collection is a most convenient locale to see where we have been and, as well, where we might go. Other works to consult include: ANAGNOSTOU (2009), DI PRIMA, GAMBINO, GARDAPHÉ (2004), VECOLI.

The Dehumanization of the "Other"

In early fall 2015, Laura Boldrini, then president of Italy's Chamber of Deputies, visited the Consulate General of Italy in New York City, and stated that over 60 million people were "in flux" throughout the world. "In flux", as we all know, is a recently coined phrase that refers, here, to the current world–wide migration that we all witness to some degree or another on a daily basis. What we see for the most part in the news concerns the more recent deluge of an exodus that occurs throughout the Mediterranean; a flow of human beings that in recent history truly has no equal, especially in the dynamics of the voyage they undergo.

A significant number of these "migrants" are coming from middle–eastern and/or Mediterranean, war–torn countries, where previous governments — despotic for sure — have been crushed and their leaders subsequently eliminated through incarceration if not swift execution. Unfortunately, what remains in those countries is a series of weak national governments that exist only because they have the protection of the military. In addition, these countries may also have the support of one or any of the major powers in the world. Of course, for the current situation in the Middle East — specifically, Iraq, Egypt, Libya, Syria, and the like — we also need to re–examine the United States decision to overthrow Saddam Hussein in 2003, an act of aggression that has had long–term reverberations throughout[7].

---

(7) On George W. Bush's failed Middle East strategy post–9/11, see, PRESSMAN.

The bulk of these populations, middle– to working–class, is left to fend for themselves. Where, in addition, religion has come into play — indeed, in no small part — no one perceived to be of the opposite faith is spared. It becomes for many, in a literal sense, a question of life and death. So much so is this the case, that those who do leave, do so in an abjectly desperate attempt to save theirs and their family's lives despite the tremendous gamble involved. Sadly, as we witnessed in the press in September 2015, Aylan Kurdi, the three–year–old boy in the photo seen around the world, and his brother, Galip, whose bodies washed up on shore, drowned, never to see another day.

The photo was taken on September 2, 2015, by Nilüfer Demir, when she worked for the DHA Agency. It is simply chilling to see a little boy's body on the shoreline, face down, with the water obviously splashing against his face. Arms by his side and feet closed up, his positioning seems almost intentional; and his red shirt emphasizes all the more this small child's lifeless body.

We have witnessed over the years infamously tragic events both in the United States and abroad. In addition to the infinite beatings of the Black civil rights leaders of the 1960s, the maltreatment of anti–Vietnam War protestors of the late 1960s and early 1970s saw the tragic shooting of innocent students on the campus of Kent State University. Known as the "May 4 Massacre", on that day in 1970 the Ohio National Guard responded to a peace rally against the U.S. expansion of the Vietnam War into Cambodia. They killed four students and wounded nine other, all unarmed, as they fired 67 rounds in 13 seconds. This event was immortalized by John Filo's photo for which he won a Pulitzer Prize for the photo of a 14–year–old runaway, Mary Ann Vecchio, as she knelt, screaming most despairingly as if to an onlooking crowd, over the body of Jeffrey Miller who had been shot in the mouth and killed that day[8].

Equally shocking two years later was Nick Ut's photo of January 8, 1972, published by The Associated Press. Known as "Napalm Girl", the photo is that of nine–year-old Phan Thị Kim Phúc, who was the victim of friendly fire. Believing the escaping villagers were enemy soldiers, the Republic of Vietnam Air Force dropped a napalm bomb on her and her fellow citizens running to safety. Her clothes were literally burned off her body; and Kim Phúc spent the next decade in and out of hospitals in Southeast Asia and in Europe for surgeries and skin transplants[9].

Like the infamously tragic events of the past caught in photos — from the above–mentioned Napalm Girl of the 1970s and the "May 4 Massacre" of 1972, as well as other photos chronicling subsequent tragedies perpetrated by humans and on humans — many indeed hoped that the photo of Aylan's lifeless body would, once and for all, serve as the wake–up call it should surely be (for Europe and for the rest of the world, the U.S. included), so that we might finally do something to end such senseless loss of life. But, as I close this analysis in late summer 2022, we see that such hope is belied by the Russia's invasion in Ukraine and the senseless loss of life that has, to date, ensued.

---

(8) Much has been written on the "May 4 Massacre". See WILLIAM GORDON's study.

(9) Of the many stories on this event as well, see TIFFANY HAGLER–GEARD.

In our desire to end such senseless loss of life, I would submit at this juncture that we need to be keenly aware of the power of language. What do I mean? At the beginning of this chapter, I used the phrase "in flux" instead of emigration, immigration, or — perhaps more desirable of the three in current times — migration, a term more frequently used among public officials and scholars these days[10].

Yet, that term, as well as the previous two, may have its negative effect. It may readily call to mind, as I believe it often does, the notion of one's stereotypical image of the so–called "illegal" immigrant who enters a country in the most clandestine of manners, and, allegedly, (a) steals jobs from the local citizens, and (b) engages in violent acts against those same local citizens. We know, instead, that recent figures in the United States debunk such biases and prejudices[11]. Thus, the demystification of such stereotypes lies in both a new awareness of the situation at hand — that immigrants have a lower crime rate — as well as in the language we use.

We need to be better aware of the power of language and how, in an attempt to be cute, if not seriously clever, we might engage willy–nilly in a linguistic dehumanization of our brethren, especially those who are forced into a lifesaving, and at the same time life–threatening, exodus from their homeland.

What do I mean by linguistic dehumanization? There are numerous examples from the past century of verbal descriptions and visual images in which the Italian immigrant was presented in a most dehumanizing manner:

---

(10) For more on labeling, see Tamburri (2017b).

(11) See Charles Ingraham.

either disposed of by being placed in a cage and dunked into a river, as we see here:

Or, more insidious one might say, being represented as creatures with human heads and rodent bodies, as we see the next image:

This, one might say, is of the past. For sure, I am speaking of written and visual representations of the late nineteenth and early twentieth century.

So, then, allow me to use a more recent example, one that has its origins in the 2016 presidential campaign of New York's neighboring state's former governor and then presidential candidate Chris Christie. In what can only be considered a patently xenophobic quest, Christie stated that «[y]ou go on online and at any moment, FedEx can tell you where [your] package is. [...] Yet we let people come into this country with visas, and the minute they come in, we lose track of them». Christie went on to state that FedEx could surely advise the U.S. Immigration and Customs Enforcement (ICE) on how to set up a system for tracking people. Well, as I have quoted *ad nauseam* with regard to similar phenomena, this recalls the 1990 C+C Music Factory's disco hit, *Things That Make You Go Hmmm*. That is to say, with his statement, Christie automatically reduced all visitors to the United States as packages, parcel post: things readily tracked in a continuum so we always know where they are.

As reported by the «New York Times», *A FedEx spokeswoman declined to comment on Mr. Christie's remarks.* The follow–up question, to be sure (pardon my sarcasm), would be, «Is a signature required?». Of course, no one from FedEx would respond. The more serious question, to be sure, is, «Has Christie, an American of both Irish and Italian descent, forgotten his roots?». The dehumanization of such commentary by Christie reeks of the above–mentioned late nineteenth– and early twentieth–century nativism, when the Italians (and the Irish before them) were treated as the fundamentally indentured laborers they were

— if not to be shunned altogether — and seen as a menace to U.S. values of the time, as we see here:

NO ITALIANS ALLOWED

On May 28, 1888, council passed a resolution to the effect that parties receiving the contract for paving E. Washington St. shall bind themselves not to employ any Italian labor.

THE HIGH TIDE OF IMMIGRATION—A NATIONAL MENACE.

While what I have outlined above are examples of anti–Italian bigoted ads and other announcements that have appeared in the earlier part of the twentieth century, sadly, such insensitive (willy–nilly) commercials occasionally pop up their ugly heads even today. I have in mind Eataly of Chicago, which ran an ad campaign for truffles. Using an oversized banner, the commercial blurred the lines, at the very least, between what some might consider the strong odor of the plant to the stereotypical lack of hygiene ascribed to the Italian, as we see here:

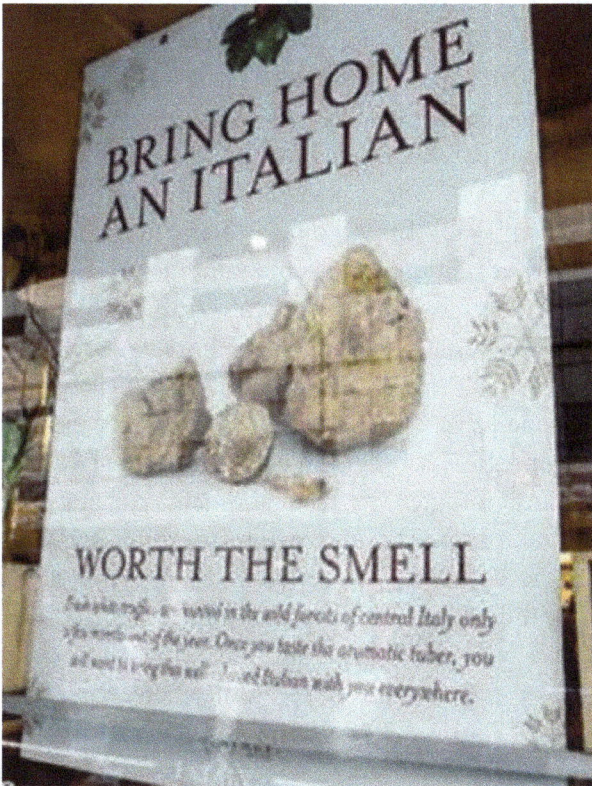

The referents here can be multiple: First, there is the stereotype of the Italian immigrant; for many Americans, «Italy was becoming the distrusted source of the hundreds of thousands of picturesque, but dirty and menacing, Italian peasants pouring into a New York City ill equipped to handle, absorb, or assimilate them» (Cosco,

23); Second, it references willy–nilly a more general physical description of Italians as Jacab Riis so infamously de-
scribed them:

> Whenever the back of the sanitary police is turned, [the
> Italian immigrant] will make his home in the filthy bur-
> rows where he works by day, sleeping and eating his meals
> under the dump, on the edge of slimy depths and amid
> surroundings full of unutterable horror (52).

Third, the phrase, "Bring home an Italian", has an implicit
ring of objectification if not dehumanization, before passing
on to the object at hand, the odorous truffle.

One question that arises is: How have we arrived at this
moment in our history, especially those of us from southern Europe, given the tragedies of the Nazi and Fascist
European regimes of the *ventennio nero* as well as, happily
so, the more progressive social and gender changes of the
1960s and 1970s both in the United States and abroad?
We in the U.S. are a nation of immigrants; we are children, grandchildren, and great–grandchildren of those
who have built, indeed rebuilt, the nation, especially after the civil war of 1860[12]. Yet, somewhere along the line,
a notion of "pure" Americanism — whatever that may be
— has risen its ugly head, obscuring, especially with regard
to those of southern European ancestry (read, Italians), the
prejudiced history in the late nineteenth and early twentieth century toward the European immigrant who came
here and dug the mines, paved the roads, and built the

---

(12) While this is not the proper place for such a discussion, this statement must be contextualized in that before the onslaught of mass immigration to the U. S. in the second half of the nineteenth century, there were the
tragedies of Native American genocide and institutionalized African slavery.

bridges: work that "Americans" of that time left to the so-called "swarthy" immigrants from places like Italy, for example, places, at that time, that would qualify for Donald Trump's 2018 categorization of "shit–hole" countries.

The Hyphen and Its Discontents

I dealt with the question of the hyphen more than thirty years ago in an essay published in a non–academic journal (Tamburri 1989). At that time, I wanted to bring light to the use of the prefix "Italo–" more than the hyphen itself. But in that writing, it became clear to me that the hyphen, as well as the prefix "Italo–", were each problematic[13]. I always felt that the use of a truncated term was questionable. Why, I thought, can people not say Italian instead of Italo–? What was it that prompted them to ignore the word in its entirety and, hence, to use a truncated form. And I underscore my use of the adjective "truncated" as opposed to "abbreviated", given the nuance of a potentially violent elimination in the first adjective set against a simple shortening in the second adjective. This difference is significant, to be sure; it underscores in the first instance an act of removal as opposed to an act of simplification in length.

Grammatically speaking, the problematics of the hyphen date back to Strunk and White[14]. Within literary criticism, however, we can start with Daniel Aaron's essay, *The Hyphenate Writer and American Letters* (1964).

---

(13) Lest we ignore the more popular hyphenated phrase, *Italo–American*, where the first term is undoubtedly a violation of the complete form of the adjective, *Italian*. in this regard, Victoria J.R. DeMara has brought up in conversation the notion of such violation as, virtually, an act of *castration*.

(14) See their manual, *Elements of Style*.

For him, the hyphen initially represented older North Americans' hesitation to accept the new/comer; it was their way, in Aaron's words to «hold him at "hyphen's length", so to speak, from the established community». It further «signifies a tentative but unmistakable withdrawal» on the user's part, so that «mere geographical proximity» denies the newly arrived «full and unqualified national member-ship despite ... legal qualifications and ... official disclaim-ers to the contrary».

Speaking in terms of a passage from «"hyphenation" to "dehyphenation"», Aaron sets up three stages through which a non–Anglo/American writer might pass[15]. The first stage writer is the «pioneer spokesman for the... un-spoken–for» ethnic, racial, or cultural group — the mar-ginalized. This person writes about his/her co–others with the goal of dislodging and debunking negative stereotypes ensconced in the dominant culture's mindset. In so do-ing, this writer may actually create characters possessing some of the very same stereotypes, with the specific goals, however, of 1) winning over the sympathies of the suspi-cious members of the dominant group, and 2) humaniz-ing the stereotyped figure and thus "dissipating prejudice". Successful or not, this writer engages in placating his/her

---

(15) It should also be pointed out that Daniel Aaron's three stages of the hyphenate writer have their analogues in the different generations that Joseph Lopreato (*Italian Americans* [New York: Random House, 1979]) and Paul Campisi ("Ethnic Family Patterns: The Italian Family in the United States". [*The American Journal of Sociology* 53.6 (May 1948)] each describe and analyze: i.e., "peasant", "first–", second–", and third–generation". With regard to this fourth generation" — Lopreato's and Campisi's "third generation" — I would state here, briefly, that I see the writer of this generation subsequent to Aaron's "third–stage writer", who eventually returns to his/her ethnicity through the process of re(dis)covery. Offering a more positive stage one, Irwin Child pres-ents a different taxonomy (1943).

reader by employing recognizable features the dominant culture associates with specific ethnic, racial or cultural groups.

Aaron considers this first–stage writer abjectly conciliatory toward the dominant group. He states:

> It was as if he were saying to his suspicious and opinionated audience: "Look, we have customs and manners that may seem bizarre and uncouth, but we are respectable people nevertheless and our presence adds flavor and variety to American life. Let me convince you that our oddities — no matter how quaint and amusing you find then — do not disqualify us from membership in the national family".

What this writer seems to do, however, is engage in a type of game, a bartering system of sorts which ignores the injustices set forth by the dominant group, asking, or hoping, instead, that the very same dominant group might attempt to change its ideas while, at the same time, it accepts the writer's offerings as its final chance to enjoy the stereotype. The danger, of course, is, metaphorically speaking, of adding fuel to the fire, since there is no guarantee that such a strategy may convince the dominant culture to abandon its negative preconceptions and stereotypes.

Less willing to please, the second–stage writer, instead, abandons the use of preconceived ideas in an attempt to demystify negative stereotypes. Whereas the first–stage writer might have adopted some preconceived notions popular among members of the dominant vulture, this writer, instead, presents characters who have already suck "roots into the native soil". By no means therefore as conciliatory as the first–stage writer, this person readily indicated the disparity and, in some cases, may even engage in militant criticism of the perceived restrictions and oppression set forth by the dominant group. In so doing, according to Aaron, this writer runs the risk of "double criticism": from the dominant culture offended by the «unflattering or even "un–American" image of American life", as also from other members of his/her own marginalized group, who might feel misrepresented, having preferred a more «genteel and uncantankerous spokesman».

The third–stage writer, in turn, travels from the margin to the mainstream «viewing it no less critically, perhaps, but more knowingly». Having appropriated the dominant group's culture and tools necessary to succeed in that culture — the greater skill of manipulating, for instance, a language acceptable to the dominant group — and more strongly than his/her predecessors, this writer feels entitled to the intellectual and cultural heritage of the dominant group. As such, s/he can also, from a personal viewpoint, «speak out uninhibitedly as an American»[16]. This writer, however, as Aaron reminds us, does not renounce or abandon the cultural heritage of his/her marginalized group. Instead, s/he transcends "a mere parochial allegiance" in order to transport "into the province of the [general] imagination", personal experiences which for the first–stage ("local colorist") and second stage ("militant protestor") writer comprised "the very stuff of their literary material".

One caveat with regard to this neat, linear classification of writers should not go unnoticed. There undoubtedly

---

(16) There are undoubtedly other considerations regarding Aaron's three categories. He goes on to discuss them further, providing examples from the Jewish and Black contingents of American writers.

exist a clear distinction between the first–stage writer, and especially that between the second– and third–stage writer, may at times seem blurred[17]. This becomes apparent when one discusses works such as Mario Puzo's *The Godfather* or Helen Barolini's *Umbertina*. More significant is the fact that these various stages of hyphenation may actually manifest themselves along the trajectory of one author's literary career. Helen Barolini, I would contend, manifests, to date, such a phenomenon. Her second novel, *Love in the Middle Ages*, revolves around a love story involving a middle–aged couple, whereas ethnicity and cultural origin serve chiefly as a backdrop. Further still, considering what Aaron states in his rewrite, and what seems to be of common opinion — that the respective experiences of Jews and Italians in the United States were similar in some says — it should appear as no strange coincidence, then, that the ethnic backgrounds of the two main characters are, for the woman, Italian, and, for the man, Jewish.

The Slippery Slope of Whiteness: Or A Means of Self–management

This seems to bring us, I would suggest, to the slippery slope (a) of the notion of whiteness and/or (b) of the desire to be white. Being of southern European origins, and as we saw earlier in this chapter, we know that historically we have not always been considered white, and as a result, those of the great Italian emigration who hailed from below the "Linea Spezia" were in fact placed into a

---

(17) In his rewrite, Aaron recognized the blurring of boundaries, as these «stages cannot be clearly demarcated» (1984–85: 13).

non–white category for a period of time. Hence, our obligation to negotiate said slippery slope seems thus inevitable; it is an obligation, I would underscore, for both the scholar and the (sometimes self–appointed) community leader. Said obligation calls for some form and/or manner of amalgamation of both sectors of Italian America. Unfortunately, the conjunction of the academy and society at large is woefully lacking among Italian Americans. This has come to the fore more recently during the fall 2017 campaign to save Columbus Day. Some recently organized groups, Columbus Heritage Coalition and Save Columbus Day, have all but eschewed any input from the academy. Indeed, a few members, in their vigor to cancel out any possible discussion and/or collaboration between the two communities, have obfuscated positions of neutrality taken by some Italian/American organizations; they have defined said neutrality within the superficial thought process of "with us or against us" only[18].

As I stated at the outset, one risk of such a discussion is to fall into a trap of flat, superficial analysis and thereby not consider the complexities of neither ethnicity nor "whiteness" as we know both concepts today. As a result, one may not recognize the multi–strata characteristic of any "white"

---

(18) For one instance, see chapter 2 herein *The Columbus Controversy and the Politics of Omission*. I would be remiss not to mention the more nuanced position taken by then president of the National Italian American Foundation, John M. Viola, in his editorial to the «New York Times»: «We at the National Italian American Foundation strongly condemn the defacing of historical monuments and expect elected officials and law enforcement to protect our public memorials from further damage so that a true conversation on their place in modern society can be organized. We believe Christopher Columbus represents the values of discovery and risk that are at the heart of the American dream, and that it is our job as the community most closely associated with his legacy to be at the forefront of a sensitive and engaging path forward, toward a solution that considers all sides».

ethnic group and therefore present an incomplete portrait
of the group at hand. As I also stated at the outset, in order to avoid this, we must force ourselves to let go of some
of our traditional historic–thematic perspectives that reign
still among certain dominant culturalists, or within what
are now nicely bleached, "white" ethnic communities. We
need, instead, to open up conversations regarding all aspects of our communities.

A European ethnic group's essentialist identification
with "whiteness" may prove counterproductive. Such
identification may suffocate, indeed eliminate, the possibility of diverse characterizations of one's ethnicity.
Especially if internal, such ethnicity would figure as an homogenous group of people who identify with mainstream
(read, WASP), when, instead, we know very well that in-
tra–ethnic tensions do indeed exist precisely because these
groups prove not to be homogenous, and on various occasions have provoked animated, internal dialogue in recent
years. Further still, identification with WASPdom may
very well lead to an exclusively «celebratory packaging of
the past [which] often forgets [...] histories of oppression
and intimidation», as Georgios Anagnostou stated (2009,
11). Such tensions were and continue to be evident in several European ethnicities[19]. We see this in the various
two–flagged, double–national hymned celebratory galas
and other such events that, if not negotiated accordingly,
may cause said ethnicity to stagnate; for it is by now common acceptance that ethnicity does indeed evolve to some
degree from one generation to the next (Fischer, 195). If
we do not recognize as much, then the consequence is that

---

(19) See Ruberto and Sciorra on a new paradigm regarding Italian identification, especially after 1973.

hegemonic past myths persist, and ethnic divisions — internal and external — arise[20].

What I am discussing here is self–management of one's ethnicity, as I have already done elsewhere (Tamburri 1991, 2014). As we know, the southern European has the option — indeed, the privilege — to identify as an Italian in one situation and as an American (read, "white") in another. This is, in fact, the privilege of the "white ethnic", which is also the conundrum of those who engage in any sort of ethnic discourse, be that discourse academic or more broadly public. The combination of and/or the shifting *to and fro* between "Italian" and "American" have, on occasion, excluded from its identification some arbitrarily undesirable historic components that may actually continue to co–buttress said ethnicity — something that is characteristic of a certain component of the Italian community in the States[21].

In eschewing said past histories, we can, without doubt, readily get caught up in a situation of diachronic amnesia for which any lack of knowledge of our ancestors' trials and tribulations during the proverbial four–decade period of 1880–1924 adumbrates such past challenges[22]. As a consequence,

---

(20) In not recognizing the evolution of ethnicity we risk not acknowledging the difference of how one generation may articulate its ethnicity vis-à-vis another. Among Italian Americans, this came home to roost with the 2010 debut of the reality show *Jersey Shore*. I would point out the following initial discussions that appeared at the time: CAPPELLI, DEL RASO, GARDAPHÉ (2010), and TRICARIO.

(21) In addition to the collection of essays edited by William Connell and Fred Gardaphé (*Anti–Italianism*), I would point the reader to Helene Stapinski's «New York Times» editorial, *When America Barred Italians*, for a more succinct history of U.S. discrimination against Italians.

(22) Documented and anecdotal, some of the past challenges include: "No colored or Italians need apply!": employment ads at the end of the 19th and at the beginning of the 20th century; Cesare Lombroso's theories adopted by USA in order to justify the exclusion of [southern] Italians; *The Skyscrapers of New*

we may fall into a state of synchronicity for which current phenomena reign and all connections to the past are lost precisely because, as a result of socio–economic progress and all that it may signify to those "moving on up", we erroneously adopt the assumption that southern European immigrants and their progeny have assimilated into mainstream America.

What we have witnessed elsewhere, instead, is that such assumptions often prove false. What we also know from some research is that «ethnicity is a process of inter–reference between two or more cultural traditions» (Fischer, 195) — i.e., different ethnic cultures — and, I would add, between two or more generations of the same ethnic group. The consequence of such amnesia may, in fact, be an inability to recognize affinities between the above–mentioned trials and tribulations of our ancestors and our immigrant ethnics today, all of which may result in a willy–nilly insensitivity toward current day immigration to the United States as well as to other places elsewhere[23].

What we thus need to do is to dismantle those long–held notions of "whiteness" and its power that aggregates

---

York (1905/06), includes the first appearance of the Italian on the silver screen: "Dago Pete"; 1891 New Orleans lynching of Italians after having been absolved in court of the murder of chief of police David Hennessy; Arturo Giovannitti on trial for murder after the Bread and Roses Strike (1912); Sacco and Vanzetti execution (1927); Executive Order 9066, February 19, 1942; the internment of approx. 3,000 Italian citizens/residents in the USA and close to 700,000 registered as enemy aliens; Mario Cuomo finished first in his law school graduation (1953) but could not get a job in a top–notch law firm in Manhattan (New York).

(23) We might argue the same for Italy. Namely, if the collective consciousness of Italy were more in tune with its emigration history of the late nineteenth and early twentieth century, one might witness a more accepting attitude to the immigrants living in Italy today. An analogous discussion might be had for the aesthetic world of migration from and to Italy. See Tamburri (2017a).

various groups into one vast cluster of, in our case, seemingly assimilated southern Europeans. Further still, we need to destabilize «white ethnicity as a bounded category» with the specific goal of «affirm[ing] commonalities and confirm[ing] differences» in order to promote, in the end, «a network of scholarly entanglements instead of isolated nodes of inquiry» (Anagnostou 2013, 122). A first step would require a greater awareness of the histories of other ethnic groups, especially those of Latinx e African Americans, for example. Second, we need to create a platform in which we can all meet and discuss both the differences and the commonalities. Third, we need to calibrate our own suffering against the backdrop of, especially, African Americans, Jews, LGBTQ+, and Women. "Whiteness" surely remains within the general conversation of ethnic discourse, but it undergoes, along the way, a series of interrogations and analyses that eventually underscore its malleability of signification. In some corners of Italian America, the ignorance of such histories, unfortunately, seems still to clamor oh so loudly.

Works Cited

Aaron D. 1964. *The Hyphenate Writer and American Letters*, «Smith Alumni Quarterly» (July): 213–17; revised in «Rivista di studi anglo–americani», 3.4–5 (1984–85): 11–28.

Anagnostou G., 2009, *Contours of White Ethnicity: Popular Ethnography and the Making of Usable Pasts in Greek America*, The Ohio University Press.

Anagnostou G., 2013, *White Ethnicity: A Reappraisal*, «Italian American Review», 3.2: 99–128.

CAPPELLI O., 2010. *Guido: A Generational Rebellion. Interview with Donna M. Chirico*, «i–Italy,org», February 5, http://www.iitaly.org/magazine/focus/facts–stories/article/guido–generational–rebellion–interview–donna–m–chirico.

CHILD I., 1943, *Italian or American? The Second Generation in Conflict*, Yale University Press, New Haven.

COLUMBUS HERITAGE COALITION, https://www.columbus heritagecoalition.com.

CONNELL W.J., GARDAPHÉ F. (eds.), 2010, *Anti–Italianism: Essays on a Prejudice*, Palgrave Macmillan, New York.

COSCO J., 2003, *Imagining Italians: The Clash of Romance and Race in American Perceptions, 1880–1910,* SUNY P, New York.

DEL RASO J. 2010, *National Italian American Foundation Official Statement: MTV's 'Jersey Shore'*, «i–Italy.org», February 9, http://www.iitaly.org/magazine/focus/facts–stories/article/national–italian–american–foundation–official–statement–mtvs.

DI PRIMA D., 1996, *'Don't Solidify the Adversary': A Response to Rudolph Vecoli*, in BONA M. JO, TAMBURRI A.J. (eds.), *Through the Looking Glass: Italian & Italian/American Images in the Media*, AIHA, New York.

DI SALVO M., 2017, *Expat, espatriati, migranti: conflitti semantici e identitari*, «Studi Emigrazione», 54.207: 451–465.

FISCHER M.M.J., 1986, *Ethnicity and the Post–modern Arts of Memory*, in CLIFFORD J., MARCUS G.E. (eds.), *Writing Culture: The Poetics and Politics of Ethnography*, U California P.

FORESTER R.F., 1919, *The Italian Emigration of Our Times*, MA: Harvard UP, Cambridge.

GAMBINO R., 1996, *Some Proposals in Answer to Professor Vecoli's Question*, in BONA M. JO, TAMBURRI A.J. (eds.), *Through the Looking Glass: Italian & Italian/American Images in the Media*, AIHA, New York.

GARDAPHÉ F., 2010, *Organized Crime,* «i–Italy,org», February 9, http://www.iitaly.org/magazine/focus/op–eds/article/organi zed–culture.

GARDAPHÉ F., 2002, *We weren't always white: Race and ethnicity in Italian American literature,* «LIT: Literature, Interpretation, Theory», 13.3: 185–99.

Gordon W.A., 1990, *The Fourth of May: Killings and Coverups at Kent State,* Buffalo, NY: Prometheus Books. Updated *Four Dead in Ohio: Was There a Conspiracy at Kent State?* Laguna Hills, CA: North Ridge Books, 1995.

GUGLIELMO J., SALERNO S. (eds.), 2003, *Are Italians White? How Race is Made in America,* Routledge, New York.

HAGLER–GEARD T. 2012, *The Historic 'Napalm Girl' Pulitzer Image Marks Its 40th Anniversary.* «ABC News», June 8. https://web.archive.org/web/20120609011057/https://abc news.go.com/blogs/headlines/2012/06/the–historic–napalm–girl–pulitzer–image–marks–its–40th–anniversary/. Accessed Jan–uary 21, 2021.

HANEY LÓPEZ I.F., 2006, *White by Law: The Legal Construction of Race,* New York University Press, 2nd edition, New York.

INGRAHAM C., 2018, *Two charts demolish the notion that immigrants here illegally commit more crime,* «The Washington Post», June 19, 2018. Accessed online February 12, 2020.

JACKSON J.B., 2020, *Dixie's Italians: Sicilians, Race, and Citizenship in the Jim Crow Gulf South,* Louisiana State University Press, Baton Rouge, LA.

JACOBSON M., 1998, *Whiteness of a Different Color: European Immigrants and the Alchemy of Race,* Harvard UP, Cambridge.

PRESSMAN J., 2009, *Power without Influence: The Bush Administration's Foreign Policy Failure in the Middle East,* «International Security», 33.4: 149–79.

RIIS J.A., 1890, *How The Other Half Lives: Studies Among the Tenements of New York*, Charles Scribner's Sons, New York.

ROEDIGER D.R., 2005, *Working Toward Whiteness: How America's Immigrants Became White: The Strange Journey from Ellis Island to the Suburbs*, Basic Books, New York.

RUBERTO L.E., SCIORRA J., 2017, *Introduction: Real Italians, New Immigrants*, in RUBERTO L., SCIORRA J. CHICAGO (eds.), *New Italian Migrations to the United States, Vol. 2: Art and Culture Since 1945*, University of Illinois Press, 1–32.

SAVE COLUMBUS DAY, https://www.facebook.com/Save–Colum bus–Day–470642106336516.

STAPINSKI H., 2017, *When America Barred Italians*, «New York Times», June 2, 2017, https://www.nytimes.com/06/02/opinion/illegal–immigration–italian–americans. html.

STRUNK JR. W., WHITE E.B., 1959, *The Elements of Style*, Macmillan [1920, 1935], New York.

TAMBURRI A.J., 2017a, *The Coincidence of Italian Cultural Hegemonic Privilege and the Historical Amnesia of Italian Diaspora Articulations*, in VELLUCCI S., FRANCELLINI C. (eds.), *Re–Mapping Italian America. Places, Cultures, Identities*, Bordighera, New York, 53–76.

TAMBURRI A.J., 2017b, *Re–thinking Labels: The 'Italian' Writer as Exemplar, or Distinct Categories as Quixotic* (afterword), in RUBERTO L., SCIORRA J. (eds.), *New Italian Migrations to the United States, Vol. 2: Art and Culture Since 1945*, University of Illinois Press, Chicago, 193–202.

TAMBURRI A.J., 2017c, *The Columbus Controversy and the Politics of Omission*, «La Voce di New York», December 17, https://www.lavocedinewyork.com/en/new–york/2017/12/17/the-columbus–controversy–and–the–politics –of–omission.

TAMBURRI A.J., 2014, *Re–reading Italian Americana: Generalities and Specificities on Literature and Criticism,* Fairleigh Dickinson UP, Madison, NJ, 3–25.

TAMBURRI A.J., 1991, *To Hyphenate or not to Hyphenate: the Italian/ American Writer: Or, An* Other *American?* Guernica Editions.

TAMBURRI A.J., 1989, *To Hyphenate or not to Hyphenate: The Italian/American Writer and* Italianità, «Italian Journal» (The Italian Academy), 3.5: 37–42.

TRICARIO D., 2010, *Guidos on MTV: Tangled Up in the Feedback Loop,* «i–Italy,org», February 5, http://www.iitaly. org/magazine/focus/art–culture/article/guidos–mtv–tangled–in–feedback–loop.

VECOLI R., 1996, *Are Italian Americans Just White Folks?,* in BONA M. JO, TAMBURRI A.J. (eds.), *Through the Looking Glass: Italian & Italian/American Images in the Media,* AIHA, New York, 3–17.

VIOLA J.M., 2017, *Tearing Down Statues of Columbus Also Tears Down My History,* «New York Times», October 9, https://www.ny times.com/2017/10/09/opinion/Christo pher–columbus–day–statue.html.

PART II

THE COLUMBUS CONTROVERSY
AND THE POLITICS OF OMISSION

When the 2017 controversy surrounding the Columbus statue in New York City's borough of Manhattan surfaced, Italian Americans from the general public expected the John D. Calandra Italian American Institute to come immediately to the defense of the Columbus statue. After careful thought and discussion with others who also administer public institutions such as ours, I decided otherwise. The reasons for which I made the decision have nothing to do with Manhattan's Columbus statue or the sign / Christopher Columbus / itself as a cultural representation for Italian Americans[1].

That said, there are three reasons, among others, that had convinced me, as dean, to have the Calandra Institute remain officially neutral on the issue of the Christopher

---

(1) As a brief aside, let me state that I believe the topic "Columbus statue" is a complex one, something that requires an attentive examination of the different statues around the country. Time, place, and who paid for the various statues constitute for me the basic points of departure for any and all discussions on the topic. Much of this work has already been done by Laura Ruberto and Joseph Sciorra (2017, 2020).

Columbus controversy. First, the Calandra Institute is a university–wide research institute. It is, secondly, funded primarily by the State of New York with tax–levied monies, which means that our funding, organically, originates from a state–wide population of people who represent a plethora of ideas and ideologies. Third, it is, essentially, a not–for–profit and hence should not engage in socio–political lobbying, as most 501(c)3 entities should not.

As a research institute, our mission is to engage in the intellectual process of investigation and analysis and present the facts of the case in question as they stand. Can we present both sides? Indeed. Should we then take a stand for one aide against the other? In most cases, as this one, I would say no.

That said, in the case of the Columbus monuments, we organized an event on October 24, 2017, around three monuments associated with Italian Americans. The monuments we discussed were: (1) Columbus statues in the United States; (2) The "Italo Balbo" monument in Chicago; and (3) The yet–to–exist Triangle Shirtwaist Monument in New York City. Five different scholars participated in the event; four represented each of the three cases: Laura E. Ruberto and Joseph Sciorra, Fraser Ottanelli, and Mary Ann Trasciatti respectively; Fred Gardaphé was the respondent. The event is available in its entirety on YouTube as "Monuments, Public Memory, and Group Identity: The Cultural Politics of Italian American in the Twentieth–First Century".

Our goal was to engage in the presentation of the facts in all their complexities, as they have been recorded throughout the respective histories of each monument. Further still, the goal of each scholar was, as we are wont to state, to complicate the matter in that s/he presented the main issues surrounding each monument, precisely because the public commemorative works under discussion are not all clear–cut cases regardless of which side of the issue you might stand or wish to stand.

Our procedural goal was, as is the case with the bulk of our activities, to engage in an open and respectful dialogue between each other, discussing throughout the event opposing or differing interpretations of these historical markers. I am delighted to say that we did so with great aplomb precisely because of the well–researched and clearly articulate presentations by each of the five scholars and, I am pleased to add, the animated and respectful contribution of the people present in our audience, a veritable full house. It was a constructive event, for sure, and by every definition of the term.

Conspicuously absent, on the other hand, were those on social media (e.g., Facebook and elsewhere) who had been vociferous in their defense of the Columbus statue and Columbus Circle. A few days later, at another event where I had laid out the Institute's policy of neutrality to one of the boisterous defenders of the Columbus statue, as I reiterated here at the outset, that very individual in question subsequently wrote the following on Facebook: "Calandra is not supporting Columbus". Now, within the context of those people and organizations who wish to see all things Columbian eliminated, to include therein the statement above is to engage in what I contend to be a dishonest act, "calumny by omission". Because this person did not accept the reasons for which the Calandra Institute had declared itself neutral on the issue, said individual decided to lump us in with those people and individuals who have taken a clear anti–Columbus stance.

Let me underscore that I do not expect everyone to agree with everything we do at the John D. Calandra Italian American Institute. But I do expect, indeed presume, that our opinions and decisions will be represented in an accurate and complete manner. This was not the case. Instead, this person set up a rhetorical situation in which the inference that comes forth from someone who reads such a statement — and, again, especially within the context of anti–Columbian discussions — may very well lead the person reading to conclude by extrapolation the following notion: «Not only does Calandra not support Columbus, but it supports eliminating him and all that he represents from history». This, in fact, was the subsequent reaction of a few people who either read that statement or was informed of it. A few days later several people approached me to tell me that they had heard some troubling news about the Calandra Institute, that it was against Columbus. This, of course, is not true, as should be clear at this juncture.

Indeed, this is precisely the danger of what I have called calumny by omission. Intentional or not, it is fundamentally *dishonest*. It is, equally so, divisive. As a result, it leads anywhere but to open dialogue between opposing and/ or differing interpretations of historical phenomena and events, which should lead us in the direction of some sort of general consensus. Consequently, for those of us who are misrepresented in these cases, we are, unfortunately, discouraged to engage further, precisely because of such seemingly vitriolic and mendacious behavior. Other disconcerting and discomforting behavior is the inflammatory use of language in which some have engaged on social media by using words such as "traitors" and "so–called" and/or "mad" professors with regard to those people who

have either questioned the validity of Columbus or con-
demned him outright.

Some may see this observation of mine as an exagger-
ation. But given the violence that exists in our world today, this is baiting in the worst of forms. We at the John
D. Calandra Italian American Institute had experienced
this in the past. I remind you of our 2010 symposium on
Guido culture. Once we had announced that event, those
who had refused to accept the existence of such a culture
and that, to boot, the notion that social scientists might
actually want to study it, used similar language against the
Calandra Institute at the time. As a result of such inflammatory language and added threats of violence, we were
compelled to have a police presence at Calandra that day.
Shameful? I would say so; we had to prepare ourselves
against the veiled threats that we had received after we had
announced the program. These were threats of physical violence, I need to underscore here, articulated by a group
of Italian Americans who saw themselves as the protectors
of all things Italian American; they emanated from individuals associated with what some might consider a major
Italian/American association!

Implying falsehoods by omission and engaging in pro-
vocative linguistic, violence baiting are unacceptable. I have
stated for years as dean of the Calandra Institute that we
can disagree and, hence, engage in discussion and debate,
but we simply cannot adopt denigration and dismissal if we
are seeking any sort of camaraderie on those other issues we
might all find troublesome. Such behavior of this sort, alas,
goes even further than that in offense. It sets up the potenti-
ality of people misunderstanding the situation precisely because the pertinent facts have been omitted.

This is, as I stated earlier, calumny by omission, and it has no room within a community of honest and mutually respectful people who have diverse opinions on different issues, because if the truth is not offered in one instance, how can we be sure that the truth forms the basis of other issues.

The bibliography on Columbus is extensive, and it continues to grow, some might say exaggeratedly so. Indeed, too numerous to tackle. Nonetheless, I would suggest, after one decides to tackle the primary sources, the following studies: Bowden, Delany, Kadir, Kubal, the essays in Mignone, the above–cited Ruberto and Sciorra, and Tamburri.

Works Cited

BOWDEN T.A., 2003, *The Enemies of Christopher Columbus*, The Paper Tiger, Cresskill, NJ.

DELANY C., 2011, *Columbus and the Quest for Jerusalem: How Religion Drove the Voyages that Led to America*, Free Press, New York.

KADIR D., 1992, *Columbus and the Ends of the Earth. Europe's Prophetic Rhetoric As Conquering Ideology*, University of California Press, Berkeley, CA.

KUBAL T., 2008, *Cultural Movements and Collective Memory: Christopher Columbus and the Rewriting of the National Origin Myth*, Palgrave Macmillan, New York.

MIGNONE M. (ed.), 1993, *Columbus: Meeting of Cultures*, FILibrary, Stony Brook.

Monuments, Public Memory, and Group Identity: The Cultural Politics of Italian America in the Twentieth–First Century, 2017, https://www.youtube.com/watch?v=3IegDtdcz Yo&t =3067s.

RUBERTO L.E., SCIORRA J., 2017, *Recontextualizing the Ocean Blue: Italian Americans and the Commemoration of Columbus,* http://www.processhistory.org/recon textualizing–the–ocean–blue. Accessed October 20, 2017.

RUBERTO L.E., SCIORRA J., 2020, '*Columbus Might Be Dwarfed to Obscurity': Italian Americans' Engagement with Columbus Monuments in a Time of Decolonization,* in MARSCHALL S. (eds), *Public Memory in the Context of Transnational Migration and Displacement,* Palgrave Macmillan, New York, 61–93.

TAMBURRI A.J. 2021, *The Columbus Affair: Imperatives for an Italian/American Agenda,* Casa Lago Press, New Fairfield, CT.

INDRO MONTANELLI: REVERENCE MISDIRECTED?

As I engage the issue of the Indro Montanelli affair, I should state that the fate of certain statues is more problematic than others. When the object of adoration is undeniably racist — if not also sexist and imperialist — as many consider Indro Montanelli, then any attempt at complicating and/or problematizing the issue is moot. This, I contend here, is the situation with the statue dedicated to Montanelli in Milan, Italy. I see it as yet another one of those "Oh boy!" or "Things that Make You Go Hmmm" scenarios.

That said, I shall not engage in any general discourse about statues: Columbus, Italo Balbo, Rodolfo Graziani, or those yet to exist, the Triangle Shirtwaist Factory fire as well as the recently erected statue of Mother Cabrini. I prefer, nonetheless, to separate Columbus from the other statues of this triad; while Columbus is problematic as symbol, Italo Balbo and Rodolfo Graziani are not, or, at least, they should not be. These two individuals were directly responsible for mass murder in Italy's imperialist campaign in

Lybia and Ethiopia, willing to do what they deemed possible for success. In Graziani's case, for instance, it meant
mass murder via the use of poison gas and the bombing of
Red Cross hospitals.

As we did in 2017 with regard to the above–mentioned
panel in chapter two herein, the John D. Calandra Italian
American Institute had already dealt with some of these issues further still in the past. On January 31, 2013, we dedicated the evening to a re–consideration of the Graziani
monument (2013). I shall leave that general discussion and
any requisite follow–up for another time and to others, for
the time being. Instead, I want to address, if ever so briefly, the Indro Montanelli issue, precisely because, to list two
reasons, (1) of the dehumanizing behavior that one human
being visited upon another, and (2) of the un–mitigated
arrogance, hubris, and smugness with which Montanelli
himself addressed the issue, once in 1969 and again in
2000.

The dehumanization of it all is paramount to human
trafficking and all that it pertains. In his 1969 television
interview on *L'ora della verità*, he spoke about the twelve–
year–old bride that he bought ("che ho comprato").
Indeed, he began his account by calling his marriage to a
child a "stupidità senza fine", a phrase more light–hearted
than not that was, to boot, accompanied by an enigmat-
ic smile, indeed a grin. He then immediately proceeded to
describe the experience with a nonchalance that has truly
no equal. Even in response to the Ethiopian–Italian journalist in the audience, Elvira Banotti, who spoke of rape
("violenza carnale"), Montanelli engaged in, to be sure, a
type of moral relativism, as he asked if the female journalist
wanted to «istruir[lo] con un processo a posteriori» (teach

him with a trial after the fact). This type of defense, let's be honest, is tantamount to what we heard about Nazi soldiers; after all, they «were only following orders».

In one of his columns for his rubric, *La stanza di Montanelli* (2 February 2000), he revisited the issue with an arrogance similar to that which he had displayed more than 20 years earlier on TV. The column is a response to a letter sent to him by an 18–year–old female whom Montanelli tries to excoriate in his opening paragraph:

> La tua domanda è alquanto indiscreta, e se tu fossi una diciottenne dei tempi in cui io ero un venticinquenne, la cestinerei senza esitare. Ma siccome sento dire che le diciottenni di oggi sono in grado di affrontare qualsiasi verità senza nemmeno l'imbarazzo di doversene fingere scandalizzate, eccoti quella mia, anche se probabilmente tornerà a tirarmi addosso — com'è già accaduto — le qualifiche di colonialista, imperialista, e perfino quello di stupratore.

[Your question is rather indiscreet, and if you were an 18–year–old girl from the days when I was a 25–year–old, I would trash it without hesitation. But since I hear that today's 18–year–old girls can face any truth without even the embarrassment of having to pretend to be scandalized, here's mine, even if it will probably come back to haunt me — as has already happened — the qualifications of colonialist, imperialist, and even that of rapist.]

Well, no! Given his propensity before 2000 to discuss this issue with such bluster and braggadocio (he did so in the interim during an interview with Enzo Biagi [1982]), the young woman's question is anything but "indiscrete"; *au contraire*, she asks him about a previous article of his in which he spoke of his «"storia" vissuta … con una "faccetta nera"» («"lived" experience … with a "little black face"»). His response, as anyone who knows Italian immediately understands, reeks, at the very least, of sarcasm. He then goes on to play the victim by complaining that he was accused of being a «colonialista, imperialista, e perfino quello di stupratore» (colonialist, imperialist, and even rapist). Well, he seems to have left out a fourth accusation, human trafficker. Yes, anyone who engages in "buying" another human being engages in human trafficking, defined by the United States Department of Homeland Security as «the use of force, fraud, or coercion to obtain some type of labor or commercial sex act»[1].

Un processo a posteriori? Well, Montanelli is long gone, and we are left with his own words — *scripta manent* — of the history of his own behavior in this case — *facta valent* — were we to opine on the matter. Further still, in so doing, we might be accused of running the risk of looking at history through today's lens. I, in turn, might concede such a notion, if ever so temporarily, were the distance in time significant; i.e., centuries–old, and I underscore the plural here. But it is not. We are dealing with an issue that took place in the 1930s, and through technology of print and visual media we are now privy to Montanelli's own words; indeed, those on video are accompanied by tone and gestures, those accoutrements of articulation that contribute

---

(1) The National Human Trafficking Hotline defines human trafficking as «a form of modern–day slavery in which traffickers use force, fraud, or coercion to control victims for the purpose of engaging in commercial sex acts or labor services against his/her will» (https:// humantraffickinghotline.org/type–trafficking/human–trafficking. Accessed January 25, 2020).

to the viewer's *potential* realization of meaning and intent of the speaker.

I was indeed surprised by three attempts to exonerate — Dare we say acquit? — Indro Montanelli by some current–day thinkers. The first two statements by two individuals here I find to be highly problematic, to say the least. On June 11, 2020, in an opinion piece for Italy's highly respected «Corriere della Sera», journalist Beppe Severgnini wrote that «[i]f an isolated episode were enough to disqualify a life, not a single statue would remain standing. Only those of the saints, and not all of them». Well, in theory, there may be some truth to this. However, as the thinkers that we are — cogitators to echo the late eighteenth–century dictum — are we not able, indeed, do we not wish, to distinguish the significance of the severity of one act vis–à–vis another? For instance, to be a card–carrying Fascist in 1924 was one thing, but to be an integral part of the mechanism of a regime that made people disappear, as in the case of Giacomo Matteotti, is another. (I ask my reader to dispense for the moment of the blurred lines of specificities, as we might be apt to condemn both on an equal level.) Let us not gloss over the fact that this apparently unwarranted, "isolated incident" to which Severgnini alludes involved Montanelli's "buying" an Ethiopian 12–year–old girl as his "wife". So, when I read Servegnini's comment, I thought, as I quote myself: *Now, let me get this straight. Montanelli did nothing of exception save to engage in dehumanizing, racist, sexually violent, and pedophiliac behavior.* This is the "isolated incident" of which Servegnini speaks! Really?

Severgnini, however, is not alone in his quest to keep Montanelli mounted on his perch forever immortalized in his own public space at the public's expense in the city of Milan. «È figlio del suo tempo», Marco Travaglio tells us during an episode of the TV program *Accordi&Disaccordi*. Following that logic, then, do we also accept the notion that "del suo tempo" were other historical phenomena such as the Holocaust and Slavery? Mine is not a rhetorical question; it asks where we draw the line, when do we decide that "history" is not a forgiving rationale. If there is no statute of limitations, for example, on murder and other crimes, how is it that «[g]iudicare i fenomeni storici con gli occhi di qualche decennio dopo non ha alcun senso» (judging historical phenomena with the eyes of a few decades later makes no sense), as Travaglio is quoted on the above–cited website? Finally, another member of this choie is the head of the Associazione Nazionale Partigiani d'Italia (National Association of Italian Partisans), Roberto Cenati, in stating the following: «without that man, today we would have Nazis everywhere». — Really? There were no other "giornalisti partigiani" or others *post–quem* running around?

Indro Montanelli was not the only victim of kneecapping by the Brigate Rosse (Red Brigades). During that same period Emilio Rossi, the then director of TG1, Italy's premiere news channel, was attacked. Also wounded in a similar affront was Vittorio Bruno, deputy editor of the Genova daily «Secolo XIX». Montanelli, so it seems, happened to be the more conservative and better known of the numerous journalists wounded and/or assassinated during the *anni di piombo* (Years of Lead); his years of public exposure both in print and on television, as well as his right–wing political leaning, surely contributed to why he was attacked. The irony, in any event, is that he became the idol for a park and statue whereas the other two I mention here, one the news director for Italy's State Channel 1, did not. Why? Well, the reasons are many, the discussion of which is more suitable for another time and another venue.

The third piece I found problematic is among the three published on the site, «La Voce di New York», «Non fare di ogni statua un fascio–razzista: Colombo non rappresenta i valori di Rizzo» (Not Every Statue is Fascist or Racist: Columbus Does Not Share Rizzo's Values) by Stefano Luconi. While there are numerous debatable issues with any article of this type — to begin with, which statues should remain and which should be taken down — I shall concentrate on that which I find related to a significant degree to the Montanelli controversy. In his first four paragraphs Luconi speaks to the racial strife we currently see around us and the statues. He decries those monuments that are clearly racist in nature, in honor of those individuals who are celebrated for their

strenua difesa dello schiavismo da parte della società del Sud. Non a caso, molte di queste statue non vennero erette subito dopo la conclusione della guerra civile, bensì nel successivo periodo del consolidamento della segregazione razziale, in special modo all'inizio del Novecento, quasi a voler minacciare dai loro piedistalli gli afroamericani...

[for their strenuous defense of slavery on the part of the Southern society. It is no accident that many of these statues were not erected immediately after the conclusion of the Civil War, but in the successive period of the consolidation of racial segregation, and especially at the beginning of the Twentieth Century, almost as if they were meant as a threat to African–Americans.]

Luconi then goes on to defend the Columbus statues as an expression of celebration on the part of Italian Americans in order to «onorare lo scopritore dell'America» (to honor the discoverer of America) and, at the same time, to underscore their own legitimacy in the United States since, especially during the period ending the nineteenth century when the Columbus Statue in New York City was erected, «immigrati sbarcati dall'Italia erano considerati indesiderabili e inassimilabili in una società protestante e di ascendenza anglosassone a causa della loro origine mediterranea e della prevalente devozione cattolica» (immigrants from Italy were considered undesirable and inadmissible in a protestant society of Anglo–Saxon origin because of their Mediterranean origin and prevalently of Catholic devotion). Okay, so I shall, for argument's sake, accept the complexities that some might see with regard to the Columbus Affair, especially for the New York City Columbus statue in Columbus Circle. (Again, I remind my reader at this juncture that the Columbus controversy is not the intention of this specific chapter[2]).

Regarding Montanelli, this is where I find Luconi's piece problematic. As I assume a good number of people might agree, Luconi concurs with many that the statue of Frank Rizzo should be removed; more than his tenure as mayor of Philadelphia, Rizzo's notoriety originates in his «pugno di ferro contro le organizzazioni degli afroamericani e per le violazioni dei diritti civili dei loro membri negli anni in cui fu il police commissioner della città» (iron fist against African–American organizations, and for the violations of the civil rights of their members in the years in which he was police commissioner of the city). Or, equally unwarranted

---

(2) For more on Columbus, see my *The Columbus Affair* (2021).

was the attack he ordered on «una manifestazione pacifica di studenti afroamericani» (a peaceful demonstration of African–American students) fifteen of whom were hospitalized. These actions, according to Luconi, place the monument to Rizzo among those that «rientra[no] a buon diritto tra quelli da rimuovere» (should rightly be among those that must be removed).

The passage from a condemnation of Rizzo for his racist behavior to reverence of Indro Montanelli, whose statue — regardless, and to his own admission, that he was, among other things, a "colonialist", "imperialist", "rapist", and, my word, racist, supposedly, «onora la libertà d'informazione e chi ha avuto il coraggio di alimentarla anche durante i cupi anni di piombo della storia italiana» (honors freedom of information and those who have had the courage to support it even during the dark "Years of Lead" of Italian history), is a gigantic step in rhetoric, to be sure. And I make this assertion of an overwrought argument precisely because of what Luconi himself states as preface to his rationale. His previous two sentences are:

> La colpa imputata al giornalista? Essersi vantato di aver acquistato una schiava sessuale minorenne mentre combatteva con le truppe italiane nella guerra fascista di conquista dell'Etiopia nel 1935. Il monumento, però, non intende glorificare lo sfruttamento sessuale delle africane, né il colonialismo italiano. Sorge nel luogo dove Montanelli fu gambizzato dal gruppo terroristico delle Brigate Rosse il 2 giugno 1977...

> [What is the journalist accused of? To have boasted of having bought a sex slave, a minor, while he was fighting

with the Italian troops in the conquest of Ethiopia in
1935. The monument, however, does not intend to
glorify the sexual exploitation of African women, nor
Italian colonialism. It was built in the same place where
Montanelli was kneecapped by the Red Brigades on June
2, 1977...]

The upshot, then, is that, as horrid an act that it is, being kneecapped by the Red Brigades for your conservative
writings overshadows the harm that Montanelli befell on
Ethiopians in his human trafficking of a minor while being
part of a colonialist and sexist regime. Personally, I'd rather
see his statue replaced by one dedicated to Walter Tobagi,
a journalist targeted and eventually killed on May 28, 1980
by the terrorist group Brigade XXVIII March[3].

Severgnini, Travaglio, Cenati, and Luconi himself es-
chew the evaluation of past events and/or behavior through
the lens of today. Indeed, Luconi tells us such phenomena
should undergo a "metro di valutazione morale coevo" (coeval moral measure of evaluation). As I mentioned earlier, we
might indeed attempt to do so with events and activities of
centuries ago, though the extremity of said phenomena and
those individuals involved just might cancel out the validity
of a "coeval moral measure of evaluation".

In Montanelli's case, I am hard–pressed not to moralize history — as Filippo Barberis, a member of the Partito
Democratico, to boot, decries doing — in this case especially. While we're here, we might indeed moralize such opinions about accepting such logic that condones Montanelli's

---

(3) I am aware that many cities have already honored Tobagi's memory.
Clearly, one more city to honor Tobagi in place of Montanelli is a moot point.
Why not do so?

behavior by the very fact that such grievous harm to another human being, a child, is overshadowed because his
conservatism provoked egregious unwarranted violence on
him by an extremist group. In this case, the kneecapping
that befell Montanelli does not cancel out his own nefari-
ous behavior of human trafficking of a 12–year–old girl. In
a certain sense, this *forma mentis* trivializes such past actions;
for Montanelli is the poster boy for all four of the above–
mentioned miscreant acts! This is not the case of a statue in
discussion, this is the case of a human being who violated,
in various ways, another human being, someone who was
physically smaller and had yet to reach an age of maturity.

In the Montanelli case we are not dealing with any a sub-
tle, hermeneutic phenomenon of difference that an able ob-
server of society (journalist or historian) should not over-
see and cannot comprehend. Since the vicious murder of
George Floyd and Rayshard Brooks in the United States,
we have initiated a discussion on whiteness and, more specifically, on white privilege. Those of us who are not Black,
those of us who are not of African origin (specifically, in the
U.S. and in Italy), truly cannot viscerally comprehend what
it means to live on the other side of whiteness. This was em-
inently clear in the case of Montanelli, as we saw in the videos and in his column; he could not see himself as the privi-
leged white, northern Italian that he was. Unless we struggle
to recognize our own white privilege, which means ques-
tioning our own "moral measure of evaluation", we shall fall
into that trap, indeed run the risk, of seeing things always
at a distance and through a semiotic lens of gender and racial privilege, which, while so doing, we do not re–cognize
and, subsequently, contribute to condoning such behavior.

Works Cited

BIAGI E., 1982, *Interview with Indro Montanelli, Questo Secolo.* Rai, www.youtube.com/watch?v=zV16EoMK9bA.

—— *L'ora della verità*, 1969, Rai, https://www.youtube.com/ watch?v=PYgSwluzYxs

MONTANELLI I. 2000, *La stanza di Montanelli,* «Corriere della Sera», 2 February.

LUCONI S. 2020, *Non fare di ogni statua un fascio–razzista: Colombo non rappresenta i valori di Rizzo,* «La Voce di New York», June 14, 2020, https://www.lavocedinewyork.com/ news/primopiano/2020/06/14/non–fare–di–ogni–statua– un–fascio–razzista–colombo–non–rappresenta–i–valori–di– rizzo/.

Rehabilitating War Criminals. The Monument to Rodolfo Graziani, 2013, https://www.youtube.com/watch?v=OZse MG9ro8A.

TAMBURRI A.J., 2021, *The Columbus Affair: Imperatives for an Italian/American Agenda,* Casa Lago Press, New Fairfield, CT.

TRAVAGLIO M., 2020, Interview on *Accordi&Disaccordi.* https:// www.ilfattoquotidiano.it/2020/06/13/montanelli–travaglio– ad–accordidisaccordi–rimuovere–la–statua–a–milano–era– figlio–del–suo–tempo–non–un– razzista/5833925/.

PART III

WHY PROMOTORS OF ITALIAN/AMERICAN CULTURE NEED TO KNOW MORE: THE ITALIAN/AMERICAN EXPERIENCE IN RELIGION

> I am convinced that there are in America today numerous young men and women of Italian origin who are proud of their heritage, not in the sense of those hoodlums who scream about Italian power, or "Italian is beautiful" and similar imbecilities, but in the sense of awareness of one's hereditary values. This can be done, provided one is willing to spend years and years digging and digging, without expectation of any reward, except the feeling of doing some good.
>
> G. SCHIAVO, *The Italians in America Before the Revolution* (1976)

I have opined — some might say *ad nauseam* — about the necessity knowing fundamental Italian and Italian/American history for those who see themselves as protagonists in the national discussion on Italian ethnicity in the United States[1]. In my *Re–reading Italian Americana: Specificities and Generalities on Literature and Criticism* (Tamburri 2014), I dealt with such notions in chapters 1

---

(1) See TAMBURRI 1991 for the slash (/) in adjectival binomials of ethnicity.

and 8, the importance of which is so vital, in my opinion, that I felt compelled to bracket my overall discussion of Italian/American literature and criticism with this exhortation. In chapter 1, I stated (2014, 4):

> [I]t is necessary that the in–group have a firm grip on the history of Italians in America: specifically, their migratory history; their development as a community herein surely through World War II; the dominant culture's treatment of Italians in America, especially before the onslaught of the 1970s' "Made in Italy". These basic literacies, I would submit, are requisite for a deeper understanding of our migratory history and its consequences for "immigration" to figure as a major rallying point. It is not enough to sing the virtues of classical Rome and Renaissance Italy to declare oneself a well–informed spokesperson of Italian America.... [T]o understand the Italian in the United States, one needs to possess an intimate knowledge of that history, regardless of his or her standing in the community.

It is very much knowledge of both Italy and Italian America that helps scholars better understand the challenges immigrants faced at the turn of the nineteenth and twentieth centuries and, further still, comprehend the roots of said challenges. All Italian Americans who identify as such, not just scholars of the field, need to inform themselves of Italian history in order to be an informed person of Italian heritage.

Given what I have just stated, and in regard to a discussion of a more performative nature — namely, when one decides to engage in activism around Italian/American history and culture — I returned to the idea once more (Tamburri 2014, 152–53), this time in chapter 8, stating that it is «imperative that [one] have a fundamental knowledge of Italy's history and how it might relate to today's world of Italian America»; and, further still, that

> the individual who claims to be in the forefront, who declares... to be the spokesperson, [s/he] needs to know all of what [Robert] Viscusi [offers his] reader in his preface and introduction [of his *Buried Caesars*]. Anything short of a solid knowledge of these facts — and how to relate then to other phenomena — is simply not acceptable.[2]

Such knowledge gaps create negative rhetorical outcomes that are embarrassing for Italian Americans within a greater discussion of US ethnicity.

One such example of an egregious outcome is contained in an article penned by an individual who sees himself as a leader of *the* Italian/American community, whatever this monolithic entity may be according to him and others who use the label so freely, especially with the anteceding definite article "the", as if there were only one *community* of Italian Americans. My contention is not with the individual per se, but rather with a particular incorrect assumption in their article. My intention is to correct a historical misconception, not to engage in any supercilious *ad hominem* attack on this individual or anyone else who makes such a claim contrary to history and current scholarship.

The article is titled *What Makes Us Italian American?* (Russo 2021a). In it, the author writes:

---

(2) I am referring here to Viscusi's book *Buried Caesars* (2006).

> We are the descendants of poor but proud people whose
> values are rooted in three essential elements, namely a
> deep and abiding sense of family, a strong work ethic and
> *a centuries–long devotion to our Catholic faith* [10; empha-
> sis added].

Notwithstanding some stylistic infelicities, I was surprised
that this statement would come from an Italian American
in 2021, particularly from someone who sees himself as
the leader of and spokesperson for major Italian American
Organizations[3]. This is especially perplexing since he
preceded the above–mentioned declaration with the statement (Russo 2021) that the «first step in being an Italian
American is learning and appreciating our family's history,
both in Italy and here in America» (10)[4].

Such a statement essentializing Italian Americans as
Catholics ignores the complex nature of Italians and
Italian Americans and their relationship to — or against
— Catholicism, especially as a religious structure of doc-
trinal guidance. Of course, class, gender, geography (e.g.,

----

(3) The author in question is the current president of the Conference of
Presidents of Major Italian American Organizations (COPOMIAO), an entity with over fifty member organizations. In the past year or so, five organizations were forced to withdraw their membership, a topic for another set-
ting. His current role was not the result of a duly contested election, as we are
wont to have. Rather, he was recommended to the membership by a nomi-
nating committee appointed by the immediate past chairperson, and then presented to the Conference members–at–large for overall acclamation, provid-
ed, of course, there were no other nominations. In my decade and one–half as
a member of this entity, there have been five chairpersons of whom only one
was the result of a true election at large.

(4) Given the propensity to engage in argumentation of the factual and
to be as precise as possible, one might prefer the use of United States in place
of America, since America is also the name of the entire hemisphere. This is a
trend, as any informed reader knows, of the scholarship at hand.

northern Italy vs. southern Italy), migration, and demographics also play a part, be it here in the United States or in Italy. It is true that more than 95% of Italians at the dawn of the twentieth century were Christians — but not all were Catholics (Data Player 2021). But it is also true that there was, at the same time in the United States, the "Italian Problem", as Henry Browne underscored. Basically, there was a concern that Italian immigrants would not be loyal to the Catholic Church and, further still, they might not support the Church as it had so desired (Browne, 52–53). In her entry "Religion" in *The Italian American Experience: An Encyclopedia*, Mary Elizabeth Brown (2000, 539) tells us that «[m]ass migration from Italy presented a possibility of a religious heterogeneous Italian community. Several American Protestants dominations conducted missionary work among the immigrants». In 1933, H. G. Duncan (184) wrote that Italy was «the least Catholic of the catholic countries of Europe... [And that a]ccording to both Catholic and Protestant estimates, between 60 and 75 percent of the Italians in the United States maintain no connection to the church». Joseph Varacalli (1986), in turn, points out that «the immigrant's ultimate allegiance [was] to the mostly non–Catholic culture of south Italy» (1)[5]. Rudy Vecoli had already discussed in detail the Italian immigrant's complex relationship to religion in his 1969 essay, *Prelates and Peasants: Italian Immigrants and the Catholic Church*. He tells us that «[m]illions of Italian immigrants and their children, it was thought, were succumbing to religious indifference

---

(5) Varacalli's 1986 revisitation of Henry J. Browne's 1946 exegesis of the "Italian Problem" is truly one place to begin one's education on the Italian American's relationship to Catholicism. From there one can get a good handle on the significant preceding essays, especially Vecoli's extended study cited herein.

and even apostasy, deserting to the camp of the enemies of the true faith» (Vecoli 1969, 220). Indeed, said problem had already been identified at the end of the nineteenth century. As Vecoli (1969, 244) tells us:

> [I]n 1886 by Monsignor Gennaro de Concilio ... profes-
> sor of theology at Seton Hall University and pastor of an
> Italian church in Jersey City, lamented that half a million
> of his countrymen were living "without any religious help
> or comfort, and do not practice any religious duty; they
> do not hear mass; they do not, for years and years, use the
> sacraments; they do not listen to the word of God" (244).

In addition to the primary texts both Vecoli and Varacalli cite in their respective essays, one might then move on to more recent studies (e.g., Peter D'Agostino, Richard Juliani, Robert Orsi, Joseph Sciorra). But regardless of what one decides, s/he should not make such pronouncements without having first become adequately informed of the matter at hand. In this case, consultation with a scholar of Italian/American studies would have set the matter straight and eliminated such embarrassing moments of what one can only assume are illusions of mediocrity. But scholars — not all, but many of the analytically engaged — constitute a group that some of the self–proclaimed leaders have decided to ignore because the scholars' expertise of the subject at hand may not always jibe with their desired alternative narratives[6].

---

(6) My use of "self–proclaimed" warrants a brief explanation. As I mentioned in note 3, not all presidents, chairpersons, etc. are duly elected in a challenged contest. Some are appointed, presented for acclamation, or simply self–declared. This is to some degree what we have in the case of several Italian/American organizations; they are sometimes managed, administrated, by those who founded them.

Were said individual truly cognizant of Italian history, conversant with many chronicled phenomena over the past 160–plus years in both Italy and in the United States — as indeed he states one should be, as we saw immediately above — he would also know that such an issue is even more complex today. Approximately 74% of Italians ascribe to some form of Christianity, with "Catholicism as the majority group among Christians"; the percentage differs in a few polls, fluctuating between approximately 72% to 83%[7]. Other denominations of Christianity include Eastern Orthodox, Jehovah's Witness, Protestant, and Methodist. Other forms of religious practices in Italy include Judaism, Islam, Buddhism, Hinduism, Sikhism. Further still, approximately 12–14% of Italians are unaffiliated and/or professed atheists. As an aside, let us remember that the National Catholic Educational Association's latest report underscores the ecumenical characteristic of Catholic schools: «The majority of families who transferred into Catholic schools were Catholic (68%), reported a household income of $100,000 or higher (66%), and were white (78%)» (1).

Richard Alba had pointed out the challenges and complexities of religion as an identifying characteristic in his 1985 (112–13) book, *Italian Americans: Into the Twilight of Ethnicity*:

Religion is inextricably bound up with the definitions of many American Ethnic groups. Irish Catholics, for example, must be distinguished from Irish Protestants, since these two groups entered the United States in different

(7) The two websites I have consulted are: "The Religious Demographics of Italy" and "Pew–Templeton Global Religious Futures Project". That there are, in fact, such demographic websites with current figures, it becomes all the more complexing that someone would get this wrong today.

periods, settled in different places, and are distinguishable in a variety of ways, from politics to educational achievements. Therefore, in defining groups to compare against Italian Americans, to chart the latter's shifting place, it is often desirable if not necessary to include religion (the religion in which a person was raised, in deference to the notion of ethnic *origins*, rather than current religion). But this seems undesirable for defining the Italian group, if only because this book concerns Italian Americans, whatever their religion. (Also, limiting the Italian group to persons raised as Catholics might bias the results a bit, by excluding some relatively acculturated Italian Americans who have been raised as Protestant.) In any event, the Italian–American group remains heavily Catholic. Over 90 percent of Italian Americans in the combined General Survey Sample were raised as Catholics, and 80 percent called themselves Catholic at the time they were surveyed (emphasis in the original).

A few observations about Alba's comments. First, his data come from The General Social Survey and are currently still available online[8]. Second, Alba (1985, 113) clearly underscores the complex nature of religion as a fundamental quality to identifying Italian Americans: «limiting the Italian group to persons raised as Catholics might bias the results a bit, *by excluding some relatively acculturated Italian Americans who have been raised as Protestant*» (emphasis

---

(8) See http://www.gss.norc.org, where one also reads, «The General Social Survey (GSS) is a nationally representative survey of adults in the United States conducted since 1972. The GSS collects data on contemporary American society in order to monitor and explain trends in opinions, attitudes and behaviors. The GSS has adapted questions from earlier surveys, thereby allowing researchers to conduct comparisons for up to 80 years».

added). Indeed, as we saw above, not only "Protestant[s]" but Eastern Orthodox, Jehovah's Witness, Protestant, and Methodist are among other Christian groups; and, I would add here, those other above–mentioned religious practices in Italy: e.g., Judaism, Islam, Buddhism, Hinduism, Sikhism. Third, in Alba's survey group, which dates from a 1975–1980 statistical portrait (1985, 109), we see that at that time, more than four decades before our author in question's declaration of Catholicism as an essential identifying characteristic, only «80 percent called themselves Catholic at the time they were surveyed»[9].

When pitted against essential declarations such as Catholicism as a *sine qua non* to evaluate any notion of an Italian/American identity, these demographic figures mentioned in the previous paragraph underscore the ignorance associated with such a declaration: *id est*, that Catholicism is one of three essential elements to being Italian American. Such a statement negates *tout court* the other 20% of Italians and all their descendants in the United States. Sadly, it smacks of both an historical ignorance and — willy–nilly — a religious narrow–mindedness of which we have had too much just in the past one hundred years alone.

Having a minimal knowledge of Italian history, one would indeed recall the Axis of Germany, Italy, and Japan.

---

(9) In contrast to the author under question's desire to make all Italians and Italian Americans Catholic, one might readily recall the tragic history of the Waldensians in Italy, which begins at the end of the twelfth century. In the centuries that followed their excommunication in 1184, the Waldensians were the victims of further social exclusion and physical violence (e.g., the "Massacre of Mérindol" [1545], the "Piedmont Easter" [1655]). For one example of Italian Waldensians in the US, see "Waldenses Settle in Burke County" (2016). For an overview of Waldensians, see Emilio Comba (1978). For an overview of Protestants in Italy and the US — including Waldensians in the US — see, Dennis Barone (2016).

Said Axis was the root evil of the desired elimination of Jews from both the German and Italian populations. In recognizing such a genocide, Italy's national government instituted the *Giorno della Memoria* (Day of Remembrance) in 2000, five years before the official proclamation of the United Nations. In New York City, that day is commemorated by the Italian Consulate General in collaboration with the Centro Primo Levi via a day–long commemoration of the reading of names of the more than 8,000 Italian Jews who were deported from Italy to Germany and killed in the concentration camps. In the fifteen years I have attended, I can think of only three Italian/American chairpersons who have attended and had her and his turn at reading the names.

Having a minimal knowledge of twentieth–century Italian literature, one should recall the name Primo Levi, a survivor of Auschwitz whose book, *Se questo è un uomo* (*Survival in Auschwitz*), became a world–wide literary classic for its harrowing description of life in a German concentration camp. Having a minimal knowledge of twentieth–century Italian film, one should recall the classic De Sica film, *The Garden of the Finzi–Continis,* from the novel of the same name by Giorgio Bassani, another leading literary figure of twentieth–century Italy. Of course, I am referring here to the tragic consequences of Italy's five–plus year enforcement of racial discrimination against Italian Jews, the infamous "Leggi Razziali" decree of November 17, 1938[10].

Why do I mention such historical elements? After all, one might retort, «We are in the United States, not in Italy!» Fair enough, sort of. Because, if you tell me that our

---

(10) There is a plethora of excellent books on the subject. To start, I would mention a few on different angles: Feinstein, Zimmerman, Zuccotti.

«first step in being an Italian American is learning and appreciating our history... in Italy», as we read in the article in question, then I should expect a certain amount of factual knowledge from you. You should be *remarkedly* conversant with the history of Italian emigration, for sure, and along with that, you should also know what followed in Italy, especially all that which pertains to World War II. After all, many Italian Americans enlisted in the US armed forces, many of whom were sent to Italy to fight Italian Fascism and liberate Italy from its shameful twenty–year reign of social and political, inhuman darkness.

That shameful twenty–year reign of inhuman darkness that we know as Fascism forced many Italian Jews and their relatives to leave Italy and emigrate to other countries; the United States is one of those countries of arrival. That said, then, do we not count among Italian Americans the likes of Emilio Segrè, Nobel Laureate, who began his US life in 1938 as a research assistant at the University of California Berkeley's Lawrence Lab? What about Lorenzo Da Ponte, who was one of the first professors of Italian in the United States? Or does his status as academic disqualify him *post quem*, given the animosity some self–proclaimed Italian/ American leaders today hold against scholars? What about Barbara Aiello, born to Italian Jewish parents in Pittsburgh and the first female rabbi ordained in Italy? What about Guido Calabresi, brought to the United States at seven years old, because his Jewish parents — the anti–Fascists they were — eventually had to flee Fascist Italy and moved to Connecticut. Further still, one might wonder about Andrew Viterbi, an immigrant to the US at the age of ten, who went on to become a communications pioneer, and whose work is still impactful in

our current digital age. And what about Stella Levi, survivor of Auschwitz who came to the United States at the
end of the 1940s? Can none of the above be considered
Italian Americans[11]? These are not rhetorical questions; let
us remember that these very individuals are, after all, those
Italians/Italian Americans who, according to Alba as we
read above, «entered the United States in different periods,
settled in different places, and are distinguishable in a variety of ways, from politics to educational achievements».
In this case we are talking about the exile of Italian Jews to
the United States, which has been keenly documented by
Gianna Pontecorboli in her book, *The Italian Jewish Exiles
in America*.

I mentioned these few of the many more who abound,
if only to underscore the diversity that these and others add
to a more complex population of Americans of Italian descent, be they immigrants themselves or children and/or
grandchildren of Italians from Italy. Hence, Jews, Blacks,
Muslims, Buddhists, Hinduists, Sikhs, Atheists, and others are all part and parcel of an Italian–descendent population and, as such, constitute a plurality of Italian/American
com–munities in the United States[12]. As such, then, we
need to redefine the notion of "Italian/American community" as a broad, diverse group of people who share the
commonalities of what is Italian in its various and sundry

(11) And those who may have converted from Catholicism to Islam,
for example? I have in mind Patricia Dunn, novelist (https://www.pa-
triciadunnauthor.com), and Maria Provenzano Singh, one of the few
women taxi drivers in New York City (https://www.bbc.com/news/av/
world–us–canada–15236154).

(12) Were we to then pass into the political realm, then we would find
ample material to discuss with regard to the substantial tradition of anar-
chists and the sort. In this regard, one can begin with the work of Marcella
Bencivenni, Nunzio Pernicone, and Fraser Ottanelli.

forms, and, in so doing, we can then be able to speak in terms of "the" Italian/American community, as is the wont of many.

Given what I have outlined above, let me say that the notion of being rooted in «a deep and abiding sense of family, a strong work ethic» (Russo 2021a, 10) is more than welcomed and is something I believe that, while not unique to Italian Americans, ties together many of the diverse ethnic groups in the United States, as well as the many types of Italian Americans. Conversely, the notion of being rooted in «a centuries–long devotion to our Catholic faith» (Russo 2021a, 10) as an over–arching criterion presented as a *sine qua non* to qualify one's Italian/American identity is inaccurate — it is simply too essentialist and exclusionary. To be clear, the application of such a notion only recalls, alas, some of the horrible legacies of religious and ethnic intolerance, be that legacy in the form of twentieth–century Italian racial laws, which were part and parcel of the Holocaust; or the victims of the "foibe", the mass killings by Yugoslav partisans, both during and immediately after World War II, of the local ethic Italian population[13]; or, yet still, in an earlier form as the Armenian Genocide.

I have put these thoughts to paper for one primary reason — a need for Italian Americans, especially leaders in the community, and scholars of Italian America to be as well informed as possible of the history and heritage before engaging in any form of all–encompassing discourse on the history of Italians in the United States, especially on notions of identity. Italian/American history does not begin

(13) In 2004 the Italian government instituted a *Giorno del Ricordo* (Day of Memory), on February 10, to commemorate the victims of the "Foibe" and the forced exodus of nearly the entire population of Italians then living in Dalmazia and Venezia Giulia, which was brought about by Yugoslavia.

with the 1891 lynchings in New Orleans, as the author in question recently stated in a letter he penned to the president of the United States as a complaint of President Joe Biden's two proclamations on Columbus Day, one honoring Native Americans, the other honoring Columbus and Italian Americans: «By effectively "cancelling" Columbus Day, you have shown that you [...] do not truly understand our story, which began with the lynching of eleven Italian immigrants in 1891 by a mob of five thousand people in New Orleans» (Russo 2021b, 1). Italian/American history begins in 1637, when Pietro Cesare Alberti first set foot on what is now New York's shores; he was followed less than twenty years later by three hundred Waldenses (Schiavo 21). That history continued with the likes of Filippo Mazzei, Carlo Bellini, and Lorenzo Da Ponte; it continues today because we stand on the shoulders of those individuals among whom we ought readily to include all non–Catholic Italian Americans.

Works Cited

ALBA R., 1985, *Italian Americans: Into the Twilight of Ethnicity*, Prentice Hall, Englewood Cliffs, NJ.

BARONE D., 2016, *Beyond Memory. Italian Protestants in Italy and America*, SUNY, Albany, NY.

BENCIVENNI M., 2011, *Italian Immigrant Radical Culture: The Idealism of the* Sovversivi *in the United States, 1890–1940*, NYU P, New York.

BROWN M.E., 2000, *Religion*, in LaGUMINA S.J., CAVAIOLI F.J., PRIMEGGIA S., VARACALLI J.A. (eds.), *The Italian American Experience: An Encyclopedia*, Garland, New York.

BROWNE H.J., 1946, *The 'Italian Problem' in the Catholic Church of the United States, 1880–1920*, «Historical Records and Studies», Vol. XXXV, 46–72.

COMBA E., 1978, *History of the Waldenses of Italy, from Their Origin to the Reformation.* Truslove and Shirley, London.

D'AGOSTINO P., 2004, *Rome in America: Transnational Catholic Ideology from the Risorgimento to Fascism*, P North Carolina P, Chapel Hill.

Data Brief: New Students in Catholic Schools, 2021, National Catholic Educational Association, Leesburg, VA: NCEA.

DATA PLAYER, 2021, *Top Religion Population in Italy 1900–2100 | Religion Population Growth*, YouTube, January 30, https://www.youtube.com/watch?v=ZoBDaCg_J7E. Ac–cessed 10 January 2022.

DUNCAN H.G., 1933, *Immigration and Assimilation*, D.C. Heath, New York.

FEINSTEIN W., 2004, *The Civilization of the Holocaust in Italy: Poets, Artists, Saints, Anti–Semites*, Fairleigh Dickinson UP, Madison, NJ.

GAMBINO R., 1974, *Blood of My Blood*, Doubleday, New York.

The General Social Survey, http://www.gss.norc.org. Accessed 10 January 2022.

JULIANI R.N., 2007, *Priest, Parish, and People: Saving the Faith in Philadelphia's "Little Italy"*, P Notre Dame P, Notre Dame.

LEVI P., 1993, *Survival in Auschwitz*, Simon and Schuster, New York.

LOPREATO J., 1967, *Peasants No More*, Chandler, San Francisco.

ORSI R., 1985, *The Madonna on 115ᵗʰ Street. Faith and Com–munity in East Harlem, 1880–1950*, Yale UP, New Haven.

PERNICONE N., 2016, *Italian Anarchism, 1864–1892*, Princeton UP,. Princeton.

Pernicone N., Ottanelli F., 2018, *Assassins against the Old Order: Italian Anarchist Violence in Fin de Siecle Europe*, U of Illinois P, Urbana, IL.

Pew–Templeton Global religious Futures Project, http://www.globalreligiousftures.org/countries/italy#/?affiliations_ religion_id=0&affiliations_year=2020&region_name=All%20Countries &restrictions_year=2016. Accessed 10 January 2022.

Pontecorboli G., 2015, *The Italian Jewish Exiles in America*, trans. Marion Lignana Rosenberg and Steven Baker, Centro Primo Levi, New York.

Russo B., 2021a, *What Makes Us Italian American?*, «La nostra voce», (October 2021): 10.

Russo B., 2021b, *Letter to President Joseph R. Biden Jr.*, October 10, 2021.

Russo N.J., 1969, *Three Generations of Italians in New York City: Their Religious Acculturation*, «The International Migration Review», 3 (2): 3–17.

Schiavo G., 1976, *The Italians in America Before the Revolution*, The Vigo Press, New York.

Sciorra J., 2015, *Built with Faith. Italian American Imagination and Catholic Material Culture in New York City*, The U of Tennessee P, Knoxville, TN.

Tamburri A.J., 2014, *Re–reading Italian Americana: Specificities and Generalities on Literature and Criticism*, Fairleigh Dickinson UP, Madison, NJ.

Tamburri A.J., 1991, *To Hyphenate or Not to Hyphenate: The Italian/American Writer: Or, An Other American*, Guernica, Montréal.

The Religious Demographics of Italy, https://www.worldatlas.com/articles/the–religious–demographics–of–italy.html. Accessed 10 January 2022.

VARACALLI J.A., 1986, *The Changing Nature of the 'Italian Problem' in the Catholic Church of the United States*, «FAITH & REASON. The Journal of Christendom College», 12 (1): 2–21.

VECOLI R.J., 1969, *Prelates and Peasants: Italian Immigrants and the Catholic Church*, «Journal of Social History», 2 (3): 217–278.

VISCUSI R., 2006, *Buried Caesars and Other Secrets of Italian American Writing*, State U of New York P, Albany.

Waldenses Settle in Burke County, 2016, https://www.ncdcr.gov/blog/2013/05/29/waldenses–settle–in–burke–county. Accessed 10 January 2022.

ZIMMERMAN J.D. (ed.) 2005, *The Jews of Italy under Fascist and Nazi Rule 1922–1945*, Cambridge UP, Cambridge.

Zuccotti S., 1987, *The Italians and the Holocaust — Persecution, Rescue, Survival*, Basic Books, New York.

WHY HISTORY MATTERS

As long as individuals continue to promote false narratives in their writings or — as in the case of the website, *We The Italians* — spread said narratives on the pretext that theirs is a aggregator of what is stated elsewhere, those who are interested in factual representation of the history of the Italian in America shall be forced to deal with the challenge of correcting said narratives.

In this brief, penultimate chapter, I shall deal first with *We The Italians* and then pass on to another example or two of how we Italian Americans can sometimes be our own worst enemies. We cannot complain about any aspect of the treatment of Italian Americans — e.g., labor issues, media representation, inclusion in non–Italian/American projects and entities — if we ourselves are not properly informed about the issues at hand. We come off as misinformed and hence ignorant of our own history.

I should also state here that it is not a betrayal of one's heritage to recognize a negative aspect of one's history. On the contrary, it illustrates one's open–mindedness to the issue in question. It also implies a lack of blind prejudice in said regard. The overall point of contention may still be made; and it would then be executed, at said juncture, in a more informed manner, for which, in the end, the initial point of defense may figure even more valid than it did at the outset.

Such was the case with *We The Italians* and its promotion of the article *The Innocent 11 and the Creation of Columbus Day*. The issues of both the 1891 lynchings and the creation of Columbus Day — "The Columbus Affair", as I have called it (2021) — is so much more complex than what we have seen emanating from the Italian/American promoters of the Genovese explorer. The labyrinthian and recondite history — that is multi–cultural and multi–lingual, to boot — makes it the overtly challenging historical convolution that it is. Yet, uninformed self–proclaimed spokespeople, who are not trained scholars and researchers, continue to spew forth historically incorrect and, as a result, ineffectual, if not damaging, discourses. We can only assume that it is the lack of regard for the seriousness of intellectual activity that moves the untrained to engage in activity of which they have very little to no expertise. This, in the end, is a basic issue we still need to confront within the Italian/American population.

That said, when an aggregator such as *We The Italians*, or any other site with a similar purpose, includes articles of a dubious intellectual and historical foundation, it has a distinct obligation to be sure that what they promote is correct. Unfortunately, what *We The Italians* forwarded by Mr. Basil Russo about the 11 innocents deviates in no small way from the truth. Equally unfortunate is that the editor of *We The Italians* sees no responsibility to fact check what appears on his website. In an email sent to me, Mr. Mucci wrote:

> This is why you're barking at [sic] the wrong tree. One thing is what is published on [sic] our magazine, or in my interviews; another one is the news section. We're an aggregator, not a newspaper, and I know you very well know that (Tamburri – Mucci correspondence).

The overall exchange was both pleasant and respectful; I mean to underscore this before I continue. That said, with our conversation proceeding, Mr. Mucci suggested that I write to Mr. Russo. But anyone familiar with Mr. Russo, knows that he is adamant in his stance that what he believes is sacrosanct. He leaves no room for debate. The very fact that he publicly pronounces that those who do not support Columbus are traitors to their heritage says it all. Of course, I declined the suggestion. Instead, my response to Mr. Mucci, in the meantime, was the following:

> I will tell you briefly why I am not barking up the wrong tree. [...]
> I understand your issue of *We The Italians* as an aggregator, as you mention. That said, you then run the risk of people assuming you are in agreement with the expressions and ideas articulated, unless, of course, you state clearly at the beginning of each piece that it is indeed a non–vetted, non–edited piece. Such a system, however, runs the risk of sending around erroneous information, which is the case here (Tamburri – Mucci correspondence).

My point here is basic. We simply cannot perpetuate romanticized, false narratives. What Basil Russo has written
in this second historically dubious article is not an opinion piece, that is an entirely different ball of wax, as we say.
He is passing off what he has written as chronicle, historical facts, all of which could not be further from the truth,
as we shall see.

First, the 11 Italians were not all murdered by lynching; several were killed by gunfire and then hung. This does
not take away from the tragic and unjust aspect, to say the
least. Nonetheless, it deviates from the facts. Indeed, the
murder of Police Chief Hennessey remains unsolved today. Some speculate that he was indeed the victim of an as-
sassination plot because he was siding with one of two fac-
tions fighting for control of the New Orleans seaport[1].

Second, what Harrison did in 1892 was by no means
the first celebration of the Columbus voyage; there was
one in 1792, organized by the WASP leaders of the very
young US, those of the first and second generation of the
Mayflower and other ships of that era; those of English origins who wanted, at that time, to celebrate the newly in-
dependent and distinctly separate nation of colonies from
the old world, *id est*, England.

In 1892 Harrison wrote the following about the second
celebration of the "the discovery of America":

I, Benjamin Harrison, President of the United States of
America, in pursuance of the aforesaid joint resolution,

---

(1) For more on the killings/lynchings, see Daniela Jäger. With regard
to taking aides, Jäger writes: «According to rumors, David Hennessy ... was
going to testify for the Provenzanos in a new trial, scheduled for October
19, 1890. It was an open secret in the city that the police force favored the
Provenzano group and that bribery played an important role» (164).

do hereby appoint Friday, October 21, 1892, the four hundredth anniversary of the discovery of America by Columbus, *as a general holiday for the people of the United States* (Emphasis added).

While we can extrapolate as much as we desire, there are two significant (read, *meaning*ful) aspects here: First, Harrison calls it the «the four hundredth anniversary of the discovery of America by Columbus», emphasis here is on the act not the agent, the "discovery of America". Second, Harrison called it a «general holiday for the people of the United States», not specifically for Italian immigrants or their progeny. Now, some may see me as anti–Columbus in stating as much. That would be mistaken. I have more faith in my general reader's judgement; I do not see most engaging in any sort of supercilious act that would place them in that category of Italians, who never truly lived in the US yet pontificate on what it means to be an Italian American — or Italian Americans, those self–proclaimed defenders of history and culture but have yet to read enough for a basic knowledge, let alone proclaim themselves as experts in the field. Of course, one would also be mistaken, especially if one's concerns are about defending a stance, rather than the more honest substantiation of a correct historical discourse and then using said history to defend a stance[2].

Further still, an act of rhetorical prestidigitation or a simple error in fact, the Columbus statue in NYC had nothing to do with the lynchings in New Orleans. The

---

(2) Let us also acknowledge that if Harrison wanted to curry favor with anyone, it was with the Italian government, which had threatened total severance of diplomatic ties with the United States after those responsible for the lynchings were never prosecuted.

author's statement, «That same year, Columbus Circle —
with its towering 76–foot statue — was constructed at the
foot of New York City's Central Park», leaves the reader to believe that the statue was constructed in response
to the 1891 lynchings. Nothing could be further from the
truth. Talk of and fundraising for the statue began in 1889
(Anonymous 1889), and its design was finalized in 1890
by an Italian sculptor in Italy (Gaetano Russo), where
it was constructed, and ultimately assembled in NYC
(Anonymous 1890):

> In the month of February, 1889, a movement was set on
> foot by *Il Progresso Italo–Americano* to erect on the fourth
> centenary of the discovery of America a monument to
> Christopher Columbus, giving it to the City of New
> York. A subscription was issued and a fund of $5,000 has
> been accumulated...
> The monument will be constructed in Italy by the fa-
> mous sculptor, Gaetano Russo, whose design was selected
> and approved by a committee nominated by the Italian
> Government.
> [...]
> The proprietor *Il Progresso Italo–Americano*, Chevalier
> Carlo Barsotti, ... has already commissioned the sculptor
> to begin his work...

Most of the money had been raised not by the nickels and
dimes of the poor working class, but by the fundraising ef-
forts of the likes of Barsotti and company. July 1889 and
March 1890 are the two dates that provide us with indis-
putable information about the Columbus statue in New
York City a good year before the tragic lynching of March

14, 1891. Chronology is obviously of the essence in this and any other history. Indeed, as one sees from this brief bibliography of newspaper articles, much of this information is readily available online and elsewhere, for which one need not even wander through the dusty shelves of any library.

* * *

Bad history of this sort leads to two detrimental ends. First, any specific argument based on erroneous narratives takes away from the overall question at hand, and hence said argument is sidelined by such infelicities. Second, in a general sense, to those who are correctly, and historically informed, such errant romanticized narratives simply make us look bad: that we are not aware of our own history.

In addition to my work in the editorial world of both Italian and Italian/American studies for the past four–plus decades, I have been engaged in scholarly research and writing in both journal venues and books. For any of us in the intellectual world of Italian/American studies, writings such as Mr. Russo's can only, at best, set us back on our heels. At worst, it discredits any discourse any of us wish to bring forth, be that discourse scholarly or of a more popular nature.

For these last two reasons especially, the factually correct needs to be underscored when we receive such erroneous writings from the self–proclaimed who are not experts in the field. In this specific case, I urged *We The Italans* to follow the events as they unfolded, and not to promulgate writings, at times infelicitous in style and rhetoric as well, that create romanticized narratives based on erroneous statements that, ahimé, assuage any sense of inferiority complex of which Giovanni Schiavo discussed so adroitly in his writings.

If one wishes to promote Columbus, one should do so. But one needs to cite the scholars in the field, those who have written on the history of Columbus and all that surrounds him. While they might be critical about a number of issues of both Columbus and those around him, they nonetheless sing his praises for the initial act of the "the discovery of America" and demonstrate how he might remain a symbol. They include, Elise Bartosik–Vélez, Matthew Dennis, Felipe Fernández–Armesto, and Robert Royal. But it takes a skilled (someone who has worked in the world of the scholarly) interpreter of these writings and others to being forth a positive discussion of Columbus, as a symbol of «new possibilities, a new world, a new time, and the re–discovery of paradise», and argue, as Heike Paul suggests, that it was the «successive Spanish colonists who supposedly destroyed this paradise and perverted Columbus's vision. His journey to the "new world" thus encapsulated "a brief moment of wonder followed by a long series of disasters and disenchantments"»(51–52).

Works Cited

ANONYMOUS 1889, *Per Cristoforo Colombo. La lista XXIII*, «Il Progresso Italo–Americano, lunedì–martedì 8–9 luglio, 1.

ANONYMOUS 1890, *In Memory of Columbus. A Description of the Monument to be Erected in this City*, «New York Times», Sunday, January 20. 16.

HEIKE P., 2014, *The Myths that Made America: An Introduction to American Studies*, Transcript Verlag, Bielefeld.

JÄGER D.G., 2002, *The Worst 'White Lynching' in American History: Elites vs. Italians in New Orleans, 1891*, «AAA: Arbeiten aus Anglistik und Amerikanistik», 27. 2: 161–179.

Russo B., 2022, *The Innocent 11 and the Creation of Columbus Day*, «La Nostra Voce» (April 2022): 1,4. Also available online: https://www.wetheitalians.com/ from–usa/innocent–11–and–creation–columbus–day?fbclid=IwAR2DMIs olgJAm3pucPVKoQC50TaiCveTpNQSfTL52Yo8O2Rew-2bZ70O8.

Tamburri A.J., 2021, *The Columbus Affair: Imperatives for an Italian/American Agenda*, Casa Lago Press, New Fairfield, CT.

Tamburri A.J., Mucci U, 2022, *Email correspondence,* April 8–9.

POSTSCRIPT

[P]eople who imagine that history flatters them (as it
does, indeed, since they wrote it) are impaled on their
history like a butterfly on a pin and become incapable
of seeing or changing themselves, or the world.
James Baldwin
The White Man's Guilt, *Ebony*, 1965.

Sei così ipocrita che come l'ipocrisia ti avrà ucciso
sarai all'inferno e ti crederai in paradiso.
P.P. PASOLINI

As I close this small voyage into this specific corner of the
Italian/American *intellectosphere*, allow me a few more examples of where history has fallen by the wayside.

Back in 2018, when the city supervisors of San Francisco
decided to change Columbus Day to Indigenous People's
Day, one newly minted Italian/American city supervi-
sor, Catherine Stefani, saw the writing on the wall, and
that the moniker, "Columbus Day", was not long for being. In the spirit of compromise, she introduced legisla-
tion for an ordinance declaring that the day also be recognized as Italian Heritage Day. In a series of comments on

Facebook, one then–president of a national organization stated: «We know what Italians did for this country, what have Indigenous people done?» When I first read this, I was astounded by such ignorance. The very adjective "indigenous" should give us pause. That someone among Italian/American leaders feels comfortable in stating as much, and to do so on a public venue such as Facebook, can only speak volumes to a combination of historical ignorance and insensitivity toward the one people who suffered genocide at the hands of those who followed in the opening of the New World.

The above–mentioned leader was not alone in such outlandish thinking. The words «Italian American life matter's [sic] as much as anyone...» is a phrase that appeared on Facebook on Wednesday, June 24, 2020, posted by a group of Italian Americans who see themselves — hence, self–proclaimed — as the primary protectors of Italian/American "civil rights"[3]. Similarly, the editor of «The Italian Tribune», a New Jersey regional weekly, stated the following in his *Open Letter to Governor Murphy* (June 25, 2020):

> It appears that you would rather support the activities of organizations like Black Lives Matter which truly spew hate and ignorance. They do not care about black lives because if they did the problems of Camden, Chicago, Baltimore, Detroit and too many others would not exist.

I am, to say the least, befuddled that in 2020, after weeks of protest over and the incessant showings of the murder

---

(3) While this is not the venue for a discussion on Italian/American civil rights, I suggest the following two studies: Fred Barbaro and John D. Calandra.

of George Floyd at the hands of four policemen, coupled with discussions *ad infinitum* on just about every talk show positioned in the center or left of center, people still seem not to grasp why "Black Lives Matter" is both valid and, to boot, a phrase onto itself.

More than a befuddlement, there is the compound confusion of it all when one goes back fifteen months within the archives of «The Italian Tribune» and finds a front–page story entitled *The Grisly Tale of Sicilian Lynchings*. In a long article decrying the "largest lynching" in the United States, which took place on March 14, 1891, and the victims were eleven Italians (a.k.a. Sicilians), the editor (the article is signed "Admin") stated the following:

> In a letter responding to an inquiry about immigration in New Orleans, then Mayor Joseph A. Shakspeare expressed the common anti–Italian prejudice, complaining that the city had become attractive to *"...the worst classes of Europe: Southern Italians and Sicilians... the most idle, vicious and worthless people among us"*. He claimed they were *"filthy in their persons and homes"* and blamed them for the spread of disease, concluding that they were *"without courage, honor, truth, pride, religion, or any quality that goes to make a good citizen"* (emphasis added).

Italians were considered «[...] the worst classes of Europe [...] the most idle, vicious and worthless people among us». This vocabulary alone should make us stop and think about how our grandparents and great grandparents were treated at the turn of the twentieth century. It is, overall, a dehumanization that truly has no equal short of slavery, the treatment of Chinese and Japanese, and the Holocaust.

And yet — and this is where the bewilderment and subsequent confusion arise — such rhetoric of one hundred
twenty–nine years ago, which I have just cited, is no different in stridency, vituperation, enmity, or loathing than
what we find in this past June's *Open Letter to Governor
Murphy*: «[They] truly spew hate and ignorance. They do
not care about black lives because if they did the problems
of Camden, Chicago, Baltimore, Detroit and too many
others would not exist». These can only be the result from,
and I repeat Mayor Shakspeare's words, «[...] the worst
classes [...] the most idle, vicious and worthless people
among us», which the editor might have well channeled.

It is especially disconcerting to see such exhortations
and statements coming from Italian Americans. Such lack
of understanding in stating «Italian American life matter's
[sic] as much as anyone» only underscores (a) an historical ignorance beyond the pale of both the United States
and of Italian immigration to the U.S.; and/or (b) a lack
of empathy for the incomparable suffering of Black people in the United States; namely, the inability to recognize
the unmitigated dehumanization of slavery and its centuries–long consequences. It tells us in the end that Italian
Americans should remain consistently mindful (*re–mem-
orari*) of their history in order to be more sensitive ("feeling") for other racial groups[4]. The very fact that the editor
of «The Italian Tribune» refers to inner–city racial tensions and the violence that "spew" forth as a direct by-
product of Black Lives Matter only signals his blindness

---

(4) Indeed, one might also wish to see a more correct articulation, however misguided the communiqué itself may be. The possessive form, "matter's",
is much too fundamentally in error to ignore. Such an egregious grammatical
error can only call into question the very message the individual wishes to de-
liver. As stated, the value of such an articulation falls flat on its face.

to, if not ignorance of, the historical treatment of Blacks in the United States. Otherwise, he must agree with Mayor Joseph A. Shakspeare when he opined about the Italians in New Orleans.

These are the more urgent historical facts that we as a nation need to revisit, if not visit for the first time. My Pollyannaish sense of hope — *Spes ultima dea* — wants me to believe that we are speaking more of the need to «visit for the first time» and of the still persistent «ignorance of the historical treatment of Blacks», and not the need to *revisit* nor the requisite discussion of one's "blindness". The second scenario is the sadder of the two, because it speaks to a sense of choice, to the idea that one had acquired some sense of knowledge of the numerous historical phenomena in question and, in deciding not to re–adjust one's thinking, has taken the specific path of placing blame entirely on the victim.

What this scenario references is Pierre Nora's concept that there are no longer any «real environments of memory», rather only "sites of memory" (7)[5]. The first would be history, the second memory as recollection. Memory, Nora writes, «remains in permanent evolution, open to the dialectic of remembering and forgetting, unconscious to its successive deformations». Further still, memory is «affective and magical» and «only accommodates those facts that suit it»(8)[6]. History, in turn, is the "problematic and incom-

---

(5) Sites of memory can be real or metaphorical. Nora in fact states: «The transformation of memory implies a decisive shift from the historical to the psychological, from the social to the individual, from the objective message to its subjective reception, from repetition to rememoration» (15).

(6) The entire passage is as follows: «Memory, insofar as it is affective and magical, only accommodates those facts that suit it; it nourishes recollections that may be out of focus or telescopic, global or detached, particular or symbolic— responsive to each avenue of conveyance or phenomenal screen, to

plete" "reconstruction" of "what is no longer" (8); it is an «intellectual and secular" act that "calls for analysis and criticism» (9)[7].

More significant here — and relevant to the two above referenced incidents — is that we are dealing with an uncoupling of history and memory, as well as the distortion of one and the other. Nora states the following:

> On the one hand, we find an integrated, dictatorial memory — unself–conscious, commanding, all–powerful, spontaneously actualizing, a memory without a past that ceaselessly reinvents tradition, linking the history of its ancestors to the undifferentiated time of heroes, origins, and myth — and on the other hand, our memory, nothing more in fact than sifted and sorted historical traces (8).

While Nora seems, on the surface, to distinguish between two types of memory above, I would contend that they are less distinguishable and more inter–reliant, indeed different facets of memory at large. Thus, in its «accommodate[ion of] those facts that suit it» (namely, the "sifted and sorted historical traces"), a memory uncoupled from history (that is, "a memory without a past", as we read above) lays the foundation for the creation of illogical pairings as we saw, for example, with «The Italian Tribune's» editor's critically disjointed pieces from 2019 to 2020, the one dealing with the lynchings of the Italians in New Orleans in 1891, the other dealing with Black Lives Matter and

---

every censorship or projection. History, because it is an intellectual and secular production, calls for analysis and criticism» (8).

(7) I have dealt with this at length in my keynote lecture, Centro di Ricerca Interdipartimentale di Studi Americana (CRISA) of Roma Tre University (2021a), forthcoming in an expanded version (2023).

all that is relevant. As we move forward, we shall see how Nora's notions of "sites of memory" and all that it pertains may help us better understand the seeming contradictions that arise from an ahistorical–based defense of monuments and similar reactions to other phenomena.

In this venue, to be precise, what I am discussing is born out of the above–mentioned televised murder of George Floyd, which was clearly the proverbial straw that broke the camel's back. The list of names — those in the near past that we have read over and over — constitute only a few of the more recent names that belong to a list of close to 14,000 Blacks killed in confrontations with the police[8].

Out of this racial and ethnic turmoil has also risen the topic of statues and their cultural valence. I mention this because my excoriation of insensitivities to Black issues is not to impugn those who defend, within this context of Italian America, Christopher Columbus as a positive symbol for many Americans of Italian descent. For the most part, those championing Columbus statues are well–meaning;

---

(8) For those who still need convincing, "Black Lives Matter" matters, for instance, because — and this is only one of the innumerable other centuries–old examples we can readily list here — of the approximately 1,000 police killings per year that befall Black men. This is the average since 2015, and as of June 7, 2020, we were on track to equal if not supersede said number: there were 463 deaths in the first five months of 2020. These are numbers compiled by the «Washington Post» (*Protests spread over Berman and Sullivan*); for reason unknown, we also read that the federal government has only tracked fifty percent of these killings. Furthermore, of the 28,301 deaths caused by direct or indirect encounters with the police, as compiled by «Fatal Encounters», 13,722 of those killed are listed as *African–American*, a tad bit over 48%. Now, one need only use these two sources as a backdrop to the last two deaths that have garnered the news media here in the United States and, finally, have led to a national discussion, as best it can evolve today, in these current–day politics: George Floyd and Rayshard Brooks. As we all now know, Floyd died at the hands of a police officer who knelt on his neck for 9 minutes and 29 seconds; Brooks died when a police officer shot him twice in the back as he was, unarmed, running away.

they believe their ethnic cultural heritage is under attack. Indeed, I espouse their right to defend their desired symbol. Through profound historical research and by way of discussions with Native Americans and agreements that may come forth, they might even prevail in saving Columbus statues[9]. But it simply cannot be done at the expense of others, especially Blacks as well as Native Americans. And I emphasize Blacks in this specific context for the very fact that there is this attempt to give corresponding value to the phrase Italian Lives Matter within the context of Black Lives Matter. Historically speaking, it simply does not equate; it is tantamount to the sifting and sorting of "historical traces" only because the Italians of 1891 suffered a similar violence that Blacks especially still suffer today[10].

***

Finally, as this book was going to press, yet another example of such blather came across my screen. In an email sent to a few thousand people, I suspect, many of us were subjected to yet another dose of ballyhoo from an aspirant, wannabe historian of Italian America. The doltish statement is: «[O]ver the last 40 years, with each passing generation, we've watched our heritage and our history gradually slip away» (Russo). No, nothing can be further from the truth. First, neither heritage nor history slip away; they are either forgotten or ignored. Indeed, over the past five decades we have watched many Italian Americans *abandon their language, history, and literature* as they moved into WASP America.

---

(9) I have rehearsed elsewhere the possibility of Columbus as symbol, representation of the Italian immigrant's characteristics of courage, exploration, and perseverance (2021b).

(10) Yam tells us that there were over 3,800 Asian–American racist attacks this past year.

As they jettisoned their heritage, they also ignored the sociological, historical, and cultural writings that continued, indeed persisted, in the face of such neglect. Therefore, if your knowledge of the facts is lacking, and your rhetoric is illogical, you simply are not in the position to make an argument. *Come si dice nel bell'ovile, l'è maiala.*

Now, it seems that some have decided to rescue, so to speak, said heritage. But they do so without the requisite knowledge that comes from, as Giovanni Schiavo has stated, spending the time «digging and digging, without expectation of any reward, except the feeling of doing some good». The "feeling of doing some good" (3), not, as seems the wont of many, "fare lo spaccone" regardless of one's lack of expertise, should be our end goal.

We should be concerned primarily with the lack of Italian/American and Italian diaspora studies in our college and university curricula. All colleges and universities that have graduate programs in Italian studies should also have, at the very least, a certificate program in Italian/American studies that can be part of a master and/or doctoral program. To date, this does not exist. This is the primary battle we need to wage. Once we begin to see such programs established, and we have embarked on the task of forming future intellectuals — historians, sociologists, folklorists, literary and film critics — we can then move on to the specific topics at hand, be those topics the history of immigration, Columbus, media representation, whiteness, labor issues, inter–ethnic relations, and the like.

But until these programs are established, and as long as those miscreant wannabes do not consult with the expert scholars (e.g., the abovementioned historians, sociologists, folklorists, literary and film critics), we shall remain stuck in this quagmire of false, romanticized narratives that, in the long run, create unnecessary internecine wars and, to boot, make us look foolish in the eyes of the non–Italian Americans who know our history better than the wannabes.

I leave you with some food for thought. The first link is to a recent piece I penned for «La Voce di New York»; it is a four–minute read. The second link is a video of the late Robert Viscusi; it is 4 minutes, 16 seconds in length.

1. https://lavocedinewyork.com/en/arts/2022/03/04/more–graduate–italian–american–studies–to–bridge–the–gap–of–our–cultural–knowledge/
2. https://www.youtube.com/watch?v=N–IbD3gLmuw&t=183s

The John D. Calandra Italian American Institute has declared itself ready and poised to assist in all ways possible; it has made such offers many times in the past to both academic units within CUNY and external non–academic Italian/American associations to no avail. But we cannot move forward in any productive way, if those who can wield influence refuse to recognize their own positionality in all of this and, consequently, do not work for the collective at large.

Works Cited

ADMIN, 2019, *The Grisly Tale of Sicilian Lynchings*, http://italiantribune.com/the–grisly–tale–of–sicilian–lynchings/, March 25, Accessed July 15, 2020.

BARBARO F., 1974, *Ethnic Affirmation, Affirmative Action, and the Italian–American*, «Italian Americana», 1.1 (Fall): 41–58.

BERMAN M., SULLIVAN J., 2020, *Protests spread over police killings*, «Washington Post», June 8.

CALANDRA J.D., 1978, *A History of Italian–American Discrimination at CUNY*, New York State Senate, Albany, NY.

Fatal Encounters, https://fatalencounters.org/. Accessed January 12, 2020.

FORTUNATO B., 2020, *Open Letter to Governor Murphy*, «The Italian Tribune, June 25.

NORA P., 1989, *Between Memory and History:* Les Lieux de Memoire, «Representations», 26 (Spring): 7–24.

RUSSO B., 2022, *A Culture in the Balance*, «Constant Contact», April 24.

SCHIAVO G., 1976, *The Italians in America Before the Revolution*, The Vigo Press, New York.

TAMBURRI A.J., 2021a, *Rememorari, or the 'Facts that Suit' Us?: Italian Americans and A Politics of [Self–] Omission*, Keynote lecture, Centro di Ricerca Interdipartimentale di Studi Americana (CRISA), Roma Tre University, October,. Forthcoming and slightly modified with the same title in BAGGIO G., BELLA M., DI MATTEO A. (eds.), *Riscostruire: i luoghi di memoria delle Americhe*, Bordighera Press, New York 295–309.

TAMBURRI A.J., 2021b, *Symbolizing Christopher Columbus? Reflections on Columbus and Italian Americans*, in Antonio VITTI C., TAMBURRI A.J. (eds.), *Mediterranean Encounters and Legacies: Incontri e lasciti mediterranei*, Bordighera Press, New York, 261–277.

YAM K., 2021, *There were 3,800 anti–Asian Racist Incidents, Mostly against Women, in Past Year*, https:// www.nbcnews.com/news/asian–america/there–were–3–800–anti–asian–racist–incidents–mostly–against–n1261257. March 16. Accessed 9 May 2021.

INDEX OF NAMES

ABOUT THE AUTHOR

Anthony Julian Tamburri is Distinguished Professor of European Languages and Literatures and Dean of the John D. Calandra Italian American Institute of Queens College, The City University of New York.

In addition to his seventeen books and more than 120 essays and book chapters, he has edited more thirty volumes. With Paolo A. Giordano and Fred L. Gardaphé, he is contributing co–editor of the volume *From The Margin: Writings in Italian Americana* (1991; 2nd ed., 2000); and, with Giordano and Gardaphé, he co–founded Bordighera Press, publisher of *Voices in Italian Americana, Italiana,* and four book series, and the Laura/ Frasca Poetry Prize.

His degrees are from Southern Connecticut State University (BS, Italian & Spanish), Middlebury College (MA, Italian), U.C. Berkeley (PhD, Italian & Spanish). Before coming to The City University of New York, he spent six years at Florida Atlantic University where he served as Chair of Languages and Linguistics, then Associate Dean for Research, Graduate, and Interdisciplinary Studies, and director of the Ph.D. in Comparative Studies, and before that he spent over a decade at Purdue University. Previous academic appointments include Auburn University, Middlebury College, and Smith College.

Tamburri is past president of the American Italian Historical Association (now Italian American Studies Association) and the American Association of Teachers of Italian. He is executive producer of the TV program *Italics*. Among his honors, he was named Distinguished Alumnus in 2000 by Southern Connecticut State University; in 2010 he was conferred the honor of *Cavaliere dell'Ordine al Merito della Repubblica Italiana* and he received the "Frank Stella Person of the Year Award", ILICA. Other awards include: "The Lehman–LaGuardia Award for Civic Achievement". Commission for Social Justice Order Sons of Italy (New York State) in America and B'nai B'rith International (Metro–North Region) (2011); the AATI Award for Distinguished Service for Colleges and Universities (2013); the "Leonard Covello Award for Distinguished Service"; and the Joseph Coccia Jr. Heritage, Language and Culture Award (2016).

Also by Anthony Julian Tamburri

Italian Diaspora Studies and the University: Professional Development, Curricular Matters, Cultural Philanthropy

The Columbus Affair: Imperatives for an Italian/American Agenda

Signing Italian/American Cinema: A More Focused Look

Scrittori Italiano[–]Americani: trattino sì trattino no

Un biculturalismo negato: La letteratura "italiana" negli Stati Uniti

Re–reading Italian Americana: Specificities and Generalities on Literature and Criticism

Re–viewing Italian Americana: Generalities and Specificities on Cinema

Una semiotica dell'etnicità. Nuove segnalature per la scrittura italiano/americana

Narrare altrove: diverse segnalature letterarie

Semiotics of Re–reading: Guido Gozzano, Aldo Palazzeschi, and Italo Calvino

Italian/American Short Films & Videos: A Semiotic Reading

A Semiotic of Re–reading: Italo Calvino's "Snow Job"

A Semiotic of Ethnicity: In (Re)cognition of the Italian/American Writer

A Reconsideration of Aldo Palazzeschi's Poetry (1905–1974): Revisiting the "Saltimbanco"

Per una lettura retrospettiva. Prose giovanili di Aldo Palazzeschi

To Hyphenate or not to Hyphenate: the Italian/American Writer: Or, An Other American?

Of Saltimbanchi *and* Incendiari*: Aldo Palazzeschi and Avant–Gardism in Italy*

Welfare comunitario
Politiche locali, sviluppo e mutamento sociale

1. Roberto Veraldi, Olga Elena Ramirez–Poggi
   Desarrollo, medio ambiente y relaciones sociales. Del Protocolo de Kyoto a la prevención y mitigación de desastres naturales en el Perú
   ISBN 978-88-255-0982-3, formato 14 × 21 cm, 108 pagine, 11 euro

2. Stefano Padovano
   Uno Sprar in Liguria. La gestione di un servizio per richiedenti asilo
   Prefazione di Ugo Frascherelli
   Postfazione di Giovanni Durante
   ISBN 978-88-255-1104-8, formato 14 × 21 cm, 188 pagine, 13 euro

3. Bruno Jossa
   Come licenziare il padrone. Dal capitalismo al cooperativismo: il socialismo democratico come nuovo modo di produzione
   ISBN 978-88-255-2156-6, formato 14 × 21 cm, 300 pagine, 15 euro

4. Bruno Contini
   Dai "lavori usa e getta" al jobs act
   ISBN 978-88-255-2132-0, formato 14 × 21 cm, 176 pagine, 15 euro

5. Elisa Matutini
   Impoverimento e strategie di contrasto alla povertà. Riflessioni a partire da una ricerca-azione in un contesto locale
   ISBN 978-88-255-3523-5, formato 14 × 21 cm, 184 pagine, 12 euro

6. Anthony Julian Tamburri
   A Politics of [Self-]Omission. The Italian/American Challenge in a Post-George Floyd Age
   ISBN 979-12-218-0284-9, formato 14 x 21 cm, 124 pagine, 12 euro

Printed in October 2022
by «The Factory S.r.l.»
via Tiburtina, 912 – 00156 Roma

www.ingramcontent.com/pod-product-compliance
Lightning Source LLC
Chambersburg PA
CBHW062101270326
41931CB00013B/3176